The Spokesma

One Belt, One Road

Edited by Tony Simpsoı

Published by Spokesman for the
Bertrand Russell Peace Foundation
Ken Coates: Editor 1970 to 2010

Spokesman 130 **2015**

CONTENTS

Cartoon: with grateful thanks to Steve Bell

ISSN 1367 7748 Printed by the Russell Press Ltd., Nottingham, UK ISBN 978 0 85124 850 9

0 (ex UK)
0 (UK)
0 (UK)
0 (ex UK)

A CIP catalogue record for this book is available from the British Library

Published by the
Bertrand Russell Peace Foundation Ltd.,
Russell House
Bulwell Lane
Nottingham NG6 0BT
England
Tel. 0115 9784504
email:
elfeuro@compuserve.com
www.spokesmanbooks.com
www.russfound.org

Routes of the China-proposed Belt and Road Initiative

LIU LUNAN / CHINA DAILY

Editorial

One Belt, One Road

The world changes, although we are not told much about it. Ships of the Chinese Navy are said to be in the eastern Mediterranean, not far from the coast of Syria, but disinformation abounds about exactly which ones. The *UK Defence Journal* asserts, ungrammatically, that 'China Have NOT Sent An Aircraft Carrier to Syria' (5 October 2015). Surely, it would be hard to mistake such a ship? As yet, China has one aircraft carrier, *Liaoning*, which was originally built for the Soviet Navy in the 1980s.

But there are probably other Chinese ships, alongside Russian ones, in the eastern Mediterranean. Certainly, the Chinese and Russian militaries have conducted joint exercises for some time now. In May, Chinese and Indian soldiers marched in the Victory Day Parade in Moscow, watched by Presidents Xi Jinping and Pranab Mukherjee. Western leaders largely boycotted the occasion to mark the 70th anniversary of the Soviet Union's part in the victory over Nazi Germany, although Chancellor Merkel broke ranks, somewhat belatedly, and joined President Putin in Moscow to lay a wreath at the Tomb of the Unknown Soldier. A few months later, in September, President Putin went to Beijing to attend another large military parade marking the end of the Second World War in the Pacific and China's defeat of Japan. Again, the West largely stayed away, although Czech President Milos Zeman attended, as did Jacob Zuma of South Africa, and President Park Guen-hye of South Korea.

Unappealing as such military ceremonials are, with their highly polished displays of might, they point to an emerging military reality in the world. Notwithstanding its claims to 'Full Spectrum Dominance' and 'AirSea Battle', the United States finds its outright military supremacy contested. The US may still spend far more on military violence than any other country, but its scope for acting unimpeded reduces. In recent weeks, the tragedy of Syria has highlighted this change, with Russian aircraft bombing extensively, supplemented by cruise missile strikes launched from Russian ships in the distant Caspian Sea. These missiles flew thousands of kilometres across Iran and Iraq, changing direction numerous times, to reach their targets.

If global military developments are increasingly confrontational, they have an interesting economic and cultural counterpart in the geopolitics of the Eurasian landmass. 'One Belt, One Road', sometimes described as the 'New Silk Road', is China's development strategy focusing on connections and co-operation among countries mainly in Eurasia. An audacious long-term project, it comprises the land-based 'Silk Road Economic Belt', invoking old trade routes through Asia, including Iran, to Europe, and the oceangoing 'Maritime Silk Road' linking Indonesia, India, East Africa and Europe via the Indian Ocean and the Suez Canal. The maps differ, but always include a lengthy branch line northwards to Moscow.

In this context, as but one example, we can interpret China's interest in the substantial port of Pireaus in Greece as part of the Maritime Silk Road. More surprising, perhaps, is the pitch made this September by British Chancellor, George Osborne, to interest the Chinese in financing and building high speed rail networks in England's so-called 'Northern Powerhouse', as well as reviving the United Kingdom's decling nuclear power programme. (Post-Fukushima, as much of the world recognises, nuclear is NOT the way to go.) As yet, the British Isles are peripheral to 'One Belt, One Road' and beyond its reach on most of the illustrative maps. But Chancellor Osborne has been quick to join the Asian Infrastructure Investment Bank (AIIB), which China has established to finance projects advancing the goals of 'One Belt, One Road'. New and improved railways will link the many countries that stretch across the Eurasian landmass. Who better to build them than the Chinese, whose network of high speed trains runs smoothly at 300 km per hour?

Of course, these developments will not have gone unnoticed by the world's hegemon. In response, the United States actively encourages Japan to jettison its solemn constitutional commitment that

> 'the Japanese people forever renounce war as a sovereign right of the nation and the threat or use of force as a means of settling international disputes.'

Prime Minister Abe's moves to do so this year have generated great unrest in Japan itself. They have also sparked heightened concern in China, where there is enduring suspicion of Japan's intentions, borne of much painful experience. In addition, the US challenges China's claims to islands in the East and South China Seas which, it alleges, threaten international trade routes. Yet China thrives on such seaborne trade, which is at the heart of its 'Maritime Road' component of 'One Belt, One Road'.

Of course, there are always alternative options, and plans may be varied as developments proceed. But 'One Belt, One Road' sets clear direction for geopolitical developments across much of Eurasia over the medium to long term. In that context, it is perhaps encouraging that Bertrand Russell's lifelong struggle for peace, human rights and the advancement of civilisation continues to find a sympathetic and interested audience in contemporary China. We relate something of his encounter with China, and his enduring influence there, in this issue of *The Spokesman*.

One Belt, One Road Timeline

In March 2015, the official Xinhua News Agency in Beijing published a timeline of public announcements about One Belt One Road (OBOR).

China unveiled the principles, framework, and cooperation priorities and mechanisms in its Belt and Road Initiative in a bid to enhance regional connectivity and embrace a brighter future together. The action plan, jointly released by the National Development and Reform Commission, Ministry of Foreign Affairs and Ministry of Commerce, offered insight into the programme's vision and endeavours. The Belt and Road routes run through the continents of Asia, Europe and Africa, connecting the vibrant East Asia economic circle at one end and the developed European economic circle at the other. The Silk Road Economic Belt focuses on bringing together China, Central Asia, Russia and Europe (the Baltic); linking China with the Persian Gulf and the Mediterranean Sea through Central Asia and the Indian Ocean. The 21st Century Maritime Silk Road is designed to go from China's coast to Europe through the South China Sea and the Indian Ocean in one route, and from China's coast through the South China Sea to the South Pacific in the other. There follows a list of major events in the development of China's 'Belt and Road' Initiative.

September 2013 – The Silk Road Economic Belt concept was introduced by Chinese President Xi Jinping during his visit to Kazakhstan. In a speech delivered at Nazarbayev University, Xi suggested that China and Central Asia cooperate to build a Silk Road Economic Belt. It was the first time the Chinese leadership mentioned the strategic vision.

October 2013 – President Xi proposed building a close-knit China-ASEAN community and offered guidance on constructing a 21st Century Maritime Silk Road to promote maritime cooperation. In his speech at the Indonesian Parliament, Xi also proposed establishing the Asian Infrastructure Investment Bank (AIIB) to finance infrastructure construction and promote regional interconnectivity and economic integration.

November 2013 – The Third Plenary Session of the 18th Central Committee of the Communist Party of China called for accelerating infrastructure links among neighbouring countries and facilitating the Belt and Road initiative.

December 2013 – Xi urged strategic planning of the Belt and Road initiative to promote connectedness of infrastructure and build a community of common interests at the annual Central Economic Work Conference.

February 2014 – Xi and his Russian counterpart, Vladimir Putin, reached a consensus on construction of the Belt and Road, as well as its connection with Russia's Euro-Asia Railways.

March 2014 – Premier Li Keqiang called for accelerating Belt and Road construction in the government work report. The report also called for balanced development of the Bangladesh-China-India-Myanmar Economic Corridor and the China-Pakistan Economic Corridor.

May 2014 – The first phase of a logistics terminal jointly built by China and Kazakhstan went into operation in the port of Lianyungang in east China's Jiangsu Province. The terminal, with a total investment of 606 million yuan (98 million US dollars), is considered a platform for goods from central Asian countries to reach overseas markets.

October 2014 – Twenty-one Asian countries willing to join the Asian Infrastructure Investment Bank as founding members signed the Memorandum of Understanding on Establishing AIIB. As agreed, Beijing will be the host city for AIIB's headquarters. The AIIB is expected to be formally established by the end of 2015.

November 2014 – President Xi announced that China will contribute 40 billion US dollars to set up the Silk Road Fund. During the Beijing APEC meetings, Xi announced that the fund will be used to provide investment and financing support for infrastructure, resources, industrial cooperation, financial cooperation and other projects in countries along the Belt and Road.

December 2014 – The Central Economic Work Conference sketched out priorities for the coming year, which include the implementation of Belt and Road initiative. Earlier in the month, Thailand approved a draft memorandum of understanding between Thailand and China on railway cooperation.

January 2015 – The number of AIIB founding members, many of which are important countries along the Silk Road routes, rose to 26 after New Zealand, Maldives, Saudi Arabia and Tajikistan officially joined.

Feb. 1, 2015 – At a special meeting attended by senior leader Zhang Gaoli, China sketched out priorities for the Belt and Road initiative, highlighting transportation infrastructure, easier investment and trade, financial cooperation and cultural exchange.

March 5, 2015 – Premier Li, in his government work report, again highlighted the initiative, saying China will move more quickly to strengthen infrastructure with its neighbours, simplify customs clearance procedures and build international logistics gateways.

March 8, 2015 – Chinese Foreign Minister Wang Yi dismissed comparisons of the initiative to the US-sponsored Marshall Plan. The initiative is 'the product of inclusive cooperation, not a tool of geopolitics, and must not be viewed with an outdated Cold War mentality,' Wang said, adding that China's diplomacy in 2015 will focus on making progress on the Belt and Road initiative.

March 28, 2015 – The National Development and Reform Commission, Ministry of Foreign Affairs and Ministry of Commerce jointly released an action plan on the principles, framework, and cooperation priorities and mechanisms in the Belt and Road Initiative after President Xi Jinping highlighted the strategy the same day while addressing the opening ceremony of the 2015 annual conference of the Boao Forum for Asia (BFA) in the coastal town of China's southernmost island province of Hainan.

* * *

'Purged by misfortune and saved by their own heroism, they deserve success. May it be theirs!'

Bertrand Russell
Preface to *The Problem of China*, November 1965

US policy towards challengers

Johan Galtung

The young US Republic, unwilling to share the Atlantic Seaboard with London, emerged victoriously in 1812 with a strong army centred in the South. Its manifest destiny pointed West, then also South, and, stepping into the shoes of the dying Spanish empire in 1898, to the whole world. Trade was needed for growth; in 1853 Admiral Perry opened Tokugawa Japan. The Japanese challenge was its closure. The Table opposite compares US policies to those of six challengers to US world hegemony: Japan, Germany, Italy, Russia, China, Islam. And Western Europe, formerly as colonialism, now as a potential No. 7 challenger. US policy is seen as five well-thought-through *proactio* and *reactio* – often ending with war or exclusion – to the challengers' five *actio*. But in the beginning there was fragmented latency, with no real threat.

Cohesion came to Japan, Germany and Italy as nation-states in the 1860s; in World War Two as an alliance. Cohesion came to Russia and China with the 1910 national and the 1917 Bolshevik revolutions; and to Islam as a Muslim Brotherhood in 1928. There was international presence: China-towns with capital, Trotskyism, missionary Islam; strong personalities.

The first US policy was positive-co-operative: the Taft-Katsura 1905 treaty with Japan (Philippines for USA, Korea for Japan); pro-Germany until the United States joined World War One victors as a latecomer in 1917; Italy steered by the mafia on both sides; investing in Russia, China; on Egypt's side in the 1956 war against colonising Israel-UK-France.

But the challengers bounced back, more

Johan Galtung established peace studies and founded the Transcend Network for Peace, Development and the Environment. He has a longstanding interest in China, which is highlighted in this schema of ten points bearing on current geopolitics.

cohesive, with challenging ideologies and even stronger personalities up front. They demanded everything the West had: colonies, access to world markets, equality. And they were blocked by the colonial powers, above all by the United Kingdom, and by the US empire.

The second US policy pitted the challengers against each other. Japan was the guinea pig: against China in 1894-5, Russia in 1904-5, Germany in World War One; now against North Korea, China and all US enemies in the new 2015 alliance.

	Japan	*Germany*	*Italy*	*Russia*	*China*	*Islam*
Latency	Tokugawa Perry	Duchies	City-states	Feudal	Ching dynasty	Colonies States
Cohesion	Meiji 1868	II Reich 1870-71	Italia 1861	Bolshevism 1917	National 1910	Brothers 1928
Charisma	Collective	Bismarck	Garibaldi	Lenin Trotsky	Sun Yat sen	Qutb
Positive	Treaty 1905	Pro-German	Clientelism	Financing	Financing	Egypt 1956
Challengers	Militarism	Nazism	Fascism	Communism	Revolution	Islamism
Charisma	Collective	Hitler	Mussolini	Stalin, Putin	Mao, Deng	Nasser
Against each other	Against China, Russia, Germany, N Korea	Against USSR	Anti-Communist	Against Nazism China, Islam	Against Russia, Islam	Against Russia, China
Total war	Firebomb Nuclear	Firebomb	Regime change	Deterred by SCO	Deterred by SCO	Islamic State?
Negative bases	Okinawa	Ramstein	Aviano	Encircling	Encircling	Confusion
'Peace'	Occupation	Occupation	Clientelism	Exclusion	Exclusion	Exclusion

Nazi Germany was pitted against the Soviet Union, but survived; with the USA joining the victors as a latecomer also in World War Two. Then, against China; but Moscow-Beijing made the Shanghai Cooperation Organisation (SCO) alliance, 1996-2001. Now both are pitted against Islam. However, imagine more Islam joins the Shanghai Cooperation Organisation?

The third US policy, if the second is not working, is total war.

World War Two was a success for the United States in Europe-Japan; the 'good war'. But now the Shanghai Cooperation Organisation deters the United States and the Islamic State seems stronger than expected.

The fourth and fifth US policies solidify victory and exclusion, with bases encircling, containing, *de facto* occupying (Japan even pays for its own occupation). Calling it 'peace' is to abuse a noble idea.

The burden of containing Russia-China-Islam now falls on the United States and on Japan-Germany-Italy, with the bases and the risks (World War Two shadows). Nevertheless, the United States also needs fighting allies. Japan, more occupied than Germany, has been forced to join the USA. The pressure will also be on Germany and Europe.

Enters Europe: Germany-France with BeNeLux-Italy, and with Brexit [if UK votes to leave the European Union], no US Trojan horse. Fearing Russia is not paranoid given Europe's three attacks on Russia. Enters Japan if the new alliance does not work. Fearing China is not paranoid given Japan's three attacks on China.

There is much for the United States to play on. However, Russia and China are strong and less vulnerable than Europe-Japan and allies; with four Islamic SCO states and a huge potential for more of the Organisation of Islamic Cooperation (OIC) 57 members joining.

Could solving Ukraine, as a neutral federation of co-operating parts with a European House on top, and solving Japan's island problems, with Russia, the Chinas and the Koreas with joint ownership of islands and a co-operative North-east Asian Community, be better than devastating wars? Also better than US policy of neither war nor peace, foregoing trade because of sanctions, boycott, the Transatlantic Trade and Investment Partnership (TTIP) – Trans Pacific Partnership (TPP) – Trade in Services Agreement (TiSA), which are closed to Russia-China?

To the United States, this spells regional mega-challenges, not single state macro-challenges. Co-operation would make NATO and ANPO [Treaty of Mutual Co-operation and Security between the United States and Japan] meaningless. The United States without alliances and bases is a USA in North America only; and Chinese 'Silk' infrastructure connects only contiguous EurAsiaAfrica. As seen by the United States, this is to be avoided at all costs. Europe, like Japan, has to be forced. Stages 9 and 10 are already in place: Okinawa-Ramstein-Aviano can be turned against Japan-Germany-Italy, dual key Nuclear Sharing Systems for European theatre missiles can be reversed. *De facto* occupation can be made *de jure* by imposing secret accords. This can all be done with very few people knowing about it. *And may already have been done.*

For the United States, this is a non-starter; being isolated, bogged down by moral costs of killing, and economic costs of bases, leaving Russia-India-China, and ever more of Islam, to the Middle East North Africa (MENA)-Eurasia of their designs, spells defeat. And both Europe and

Japan will, sooner or later, revolt.

The time has come for an agonising reappraisal: join Germany, Japan and their neighbours for co-operation and peace with Russia-China-Islam.

The state system is waning; regions are waxing. Make them peaceful.

Source:https://www.transcend.org/tms/2015/09/us-policy-toward-challengers-10-points/

Bertie and the Pagoda

'When I lived in China, I found the Chinese sense of humour extraordinarily congenial to me, and in fact it gave me great delight. I will give one instance. One rather hot day, two Chinese businessmen, both of them somewhat corpulent, invited me to spend a day in the country motoring with them. We went to visit a very famous, very ancient pagoda, which was in a somewhat dilapidated condition. There was a staircase up to the top and I went up, expecting them to follow me, but when I reached the top I saw them below in earnest conversation. When I got down again I said, 'Why didn't you come up?' And they said, 'Well, we debated with many very serious arguments pro and con, whether we should come up or whether we should not. But we decided that as the pagoda might at any moment crumble, it would be as well there should be some to bear witness how the philosopher died. And of course the whole truth was simply that the weather was hot and they were fat.'

Transcribed from Bertrand Russell's own audio recording

Chairman Mao with Zhang Yuanji,
who established Commercial Press as a publishing house.

China and Russell

Tony Simpson

The Commercial Press, Bertrand Russell's publisher in China for almost a century, will mark the 120th anniversary of its establishment in 2017. As part of its preparations, Commercial Press kindly invited the Russell Foundation to make a presentation to editors about Russell's visit to China in 1920-21, and how it impacted on Russell's worldview and subsequent actions. The Spokesman *visited Commercial Press at their offices in central Beijing, whence they travelled south to the Western Lake at Hangzhou, which so impressed Russell and Dora on their arrival in China, 95 years earlier.*

'I should love to go to China,' Bertrand Russell wrote to Lucy Donnelly, an American friend, in July 1915. Five years later, in autumn 1920, Russell arrived in Shanghai with Dora Black, a young companion from England. The intervening years marked a turning point in Russell's long and eventful life, from the personal to the public, as Nicholas Griffin has characterised it.*

In November 1918, the long and terrible First World War, which Russell had opposed from the outset, had ended rather suddenly. The high hopes of the Bolshevik Revolution of the previous year, which Russell initially shared, had given way to civil war and famine in Russia. Russell saw this cruel suffering at first hand when he joined a Labour Party delegation to Russia in May 1920. During six weeks, they travelled extensively in the vast country, visiting Petrograd (St Petersburg), Moscow, Nizhny Novgorod, and sailing down the River Volga as far as Astrakhan on the Caspian Sea. Russell met Lenin, Trotsky and Gorky. A committed socialist himself, Russell was profoundly sceptical that Bolshevism would endure and that 'by this method a stable or desirable form of Socialism can be established'.**

Out of the blue, on 30 June 1920 on return to London, Russell found an invitation to lecture in China. In a matter of weeks, he had decided to accept. How was it that Russell was invited to China at this time?

For several decades, a trickle of students from China had been studying abroad and looking outwards for guidance about their country's political and economic

Zhang Yuanji's memorial at Commercial Press, Beijing

development. This process gathered pace with the collapse of the Qing dynasty in 1911. It was accelerated further by the First World War and what followed. The old order was passing.

On 4 May 1919 in Beijing, demonstrations were triggered by developments far away at the Paris Peace Conference. It became clear that, following the Allies' victory, China would not recover sovereignty over the parts of Shandong Province that had been previously colonised by defeated Germany. Instead, they would be handed to Japan. On that day, some 3,000 students gathered in central Beijing and marched to the house of a government minister closely associated with Japan. The demonstrators broke in, destroyed the house, and some of them badly beat a visiting official. As Rana Mitter*** points out, the student demonstration of 4 May 1919 came to symbolise a much wider shift in Chinese society and politics:

> 'The new republic had been declared less than eight years earlier, yet already the country seemed to be falling apart because of imperialist pressure from outside and warlord government within China that had destroyed its fragile parliamentary democracy. The May Fourth Movement, as it became known, was associated closely with the "New Culture" which intellectuals and radical thinkers proposed for China, to be underpinned by the twin panaceas of "Mr Science" and "Mr Democracy".'

It was in the wake of such events that Liang Qichao, the distinguished journalist, political activist and founder of the Chinese Lecture Association, had suggested that Russell be invited to China. In this he was strongly supported by Mr Zhang Yuanji, who was in charge of The Commercial Press based in Shanghai. Commercial Press put up a considerable sum of money, some 5,000 yuan or £2,000, to pay for the trip. Russell's invitation was handwritten by Fu Tong, Professor of Philosophy, on letterhead of The Government University, Peking (see illustration), and sent care of Fu's old Professor in England, J H Muirhead:

> 'Will you kindly ask Mr Bertrand Russell for me whether he can accept such an invitation as to come to China for a year to give us some lectures.'

Bertrand Russell and Dora Black in China

Russell and Dora duly arrived in China whilst this huge country was in the midst of great changes and seeking direction. Science and democracy were high on Russell's list of personal priorities; democracy in the workplace figured centrally in Russell's quest for creative impulses as described in *Principles of Social Reconstruction*, written in 1915 in response to the unfolding horrors of the First World War, delivered early in 1916, and first published that year under the same title. Had this work been noticed by Chinese scholars?

In his invitation, Professor Fu wrote:

> 'Mr John Dewey has promised to lecture here for another year, and Mr Henri Bergson will come in two years' time. The former has been lecturing on the three great philosophers of our day, "James, Bergson and Russell".'

Fu added that there was an 'earnest desire among the young' to know the 'tendencies' of philosophy and science in the West, and that, as far as he knew, Russell's political views would be 'greatly welcome to us'. Fu felt the need to write care of Muirhead because, although he had seen Russell at a conference the previous year, Russell had left before Fu had a chance to introduce himself.

William James' inclusion in this trio of 'great philosophers' may surprise some readers. It suggests, in part, the significance of the recent war as Russell's invitation to China was prepared in 1920. Russell had cited James' 'admirable' address on 'The Moral Equivalent of War' in

1189

北 京 大 學
THE GOVERNMENT UNIVERSITY.
PEKING, CHINA.

Telephone Nos. 674, 633, and 632 East

191

Dear Professor Muirhead,

Will you kindly ask Mr Bertrand Russell for me whether he can accept such an invitation as to come to China for a year to give us some lectures? The reward will be about £2000, besides travelling expenses of both ways.

Mr John Dewey has promised to lecture here for another year, and Mr Henri Bergson will come in two years' time. The former has been lecturing on "the three great philosophers of our day": James, Bergson, and Russell. There is a very earnest desire among the young to learn the tendencies of the recent philosophy and science. The choice of the subjects of the lectures will be chiefly left to Mr Bertrand Russell. We can easily arrange that when he arrives his political views will be, so far as I know, greatly welcome to us. The best way for him to come will be the Suez canal route. He will be met on board as soon as he arrives

北 京 大 學
THE GOVERNMENT UNIVERSITY.
PEKING, CHINA.

Telephone Nos. 674, 633, and 632 East

191

Shanghai. If he can come in the immediate future perhaps he will not mind wiring us about his acceptance of our invitation, so as to enable us to prepare.

He is one of the very few British philosophers whom I have not made the acquaintance with. I saw him last Summer at our Joint Conference but as I did not think he would leave the conference so soon I did not talk to him. Therefore I am not in the position of writing to him directly. If it be less trouble for you to correspond directly perhaps we can do so by means of your kindly introduction.

I have an idea of inviting R. Tagore, but I shall not start doing that before I hear about this.

With best wishes,

Yours very sincerely,

T. Fu.

Principles of Social Reconstruction:

> 'His statement of the problem could not be bettered; and so far as I know, he is the only writer who has faced the problem adequately. But his solution is not adequate; perhaps no adequate solution is possible.'

Russell himself was seeking more adequate solutions in avoiding recourse to war. In this connection, his visit to China appears to have shifted significantly his outlook from a Eurocentric to a global perspective, which he retained for the rest of his long life. His nine months in the country, from October 1920 to July 1921, proved to be something of a transformative experience.

At the National University of Peking

Russell's first impressions of China and its people were favourable. As he wrote later in his *Autobiography*, he and Dora

> 'were somewhat surprised by their wit and fluency. I had not realised until then that a civilised Chinese is the most civilised person in the world … Our Chinese friends took us for two days to Hangchow [Hangzhou] to see the Western Lake. The first day we went round it by boat, and the second day in chairs. It was marvellously beautiful, with the beauty of ancient civilisation, surpassing even that of Italy.'

With the passage of decades, Russell clearly had good memories of his extended stay in China, as reflected in another passage from his *Autobiography* (p363):

> 'Many Chinese have that refinement of humour which consists in enjoying a joke more when the other person cannot see it. As I was leaving Peking a Chinese friend gave me a long classical passage microscopically engraved by hand on a very small surface; he also gave me the same passage written out in exquisite calligraphy. When I asked what it said, he replied: "Ask Professor Giles when you get home". I took his advice, and found that it was "The Consultation of the Wizard", in which the wizard merely advises his clients to do whatever they like. He was poking fun at me because I always refused to give advice to the Chinese as to their immediate political difficulties.'

Russell wrote his preface to Analysis of the Mind *whilst in Beijing.*

'There are a few allusions to China in this book, all of which were written before I had been to China, and are not intended to be taken by the reader as geographically accurate. I used "China" merely as a synonym for "a distant country", when I wanted illustrations of unfamiliar things.'

Russell Monthly (*above) also began to appear in 1920, published by Commercial Press.*

Many Chinese desperately wanted clear advice. And the import of Russell's intervention in China continues to be debated to this day, as I found on a visit to Zhejiang University where historians and classicists probed the legacy. Notwithstanding 'The Consultation of the Wizard', in his farewell address Russell did venture some broad opinions about what he had learnt during his stay in China:

> 'Two things of a very general nature seem to me evident: the first that it is not to be desired that China should adopt the civilisation of Europe in its entirety; the second, that the traditional civilisation of China is inadequate to present needs and must give way to something radically new.'

Russell affirmed:

> 'I am convinced that China, in the future as in the past, has a distinctive contribution to make to civilisation, and something more than mere quantity to add to the world's mental possessions.'

He emphasised that:

> '… a radical and permanent solution must depend upon education … It must be universal and it must be scientific and the science must not be merely theoretical, but in close touch with modern industry and economics.'

Russell recognised that it would take a generation or more for China to develop an effective system of mass education. By contrast, he anticipated that China's 'industrial resources will lead in the near future to the great development of industrialism', warning that:

> 'All the Great Powers are anxious to secure a share in the exploitation of your resources, and unless you develop more national strength than you have hitherto shown, you will be unable to withstand aggressions fomented by foreign industrialists.'

Somewhat surprisingly to modern readers, Russell urged the development of 'active patriotism' in China. He added:

> 'If your independence is to be preserved, it is necessary to transfer to the nation the kind of devotion which has hitherto been given to the family.'

Russell posed one question which he found 'on the lips of almost all the thoughtful Chinese whom I have met':

> 'How can we develop industry without at the same time developing capitalism and all its evils?'

Russell urged that the political problem be addressed before the economic one:

> 'Political reform in China cannot for many years to come take the form of democracy after the Western model. Democracy presupposes a population that can read and write and that has some degree of knowledge as to political affairs. These conditions cannot be satisfied in China until at least a generation after the establishment of a government devoted to the public welfare. You will have to pass through a stage analogous to that of the dictatorship of the communist party in Russia, because it is only by some such means that the necessary education of the people can be carried through, and the non-capitalistic development of industry effected. The Russian Bolsheviks, as is natural to pioneers, have made many mistakes, more especially in the measures which antagonised the peasants. They are now, very wisely, repealing these measures, and those who follow them on the same road will be able to profit by their experience.'

In this issue of *The Spokesman* we reprint in full Russell's farewell address as it sums up his experiences in China and Russia in 1920-21. These were controversial topics. Amongst many people who heard Russell speak during his time in China was Mao Tse-tung who, like others hungry for change, could also read Russell's lectures and speeches in a new journal, *Russell Monthly*, published by Commercial Press. In October 1920 whilst visiting Changsha in Hunan Province, Russell had given lectures on Bolshevism, Communism, and Russia. Mao was not at all persuaded by Russell's view. He wrote:

> 'In his lecture in Changsha, Russell … took a position in favour of communism but against the dictatorship of the workers and peasants. He said that one should employ the method of education to change the consciousness of the propertied classes, and that in this way it would be necessary to limit freedom or to have recourse to war and bloody revolution … My objections to Russell's viewpoint can be stated in a few words: "This is all very well as a theory, but it is unfeasible in practice".'

By the time he gave his farewell address in July 1921, Russell was indeed speaking of China passing through 'a stage analogous to that of the dictatorship of the communist party in Russia' for the purposes of education and non-capitalistic industrialisation.

Russell also lectured on relativity at Peking University in 1921, the year that Albert Einstein was awarded the Nobel Prize for Physics. Einstein had published his theory of general relativity in 1915, and Russell's lectures helped generate great interest, not least in Einstein's own forthcoming visit to China. Unfortunately, for a variety of reasons, Einstein had to curtail his visit to the 'cradle of East Asian civilisation', as he described it, and stayed

Albert Einstein followed Russell to China in 1922, albeit briefly.

in Shanghai only a few days, in late 1922 and early 1923, although long enough to be told by the Swedish consul that he had been awarded the Nobel Prize. As a result, as Hu Danian of Yale University has written:

> 'Mass publications, including books, translated books, journal articles, and news reports on the theory of relativity and its author were produced in China within a short period of time. Consequently the theory of relativity was not only quickly introduced into China, but also widely disseminated in the early 1920s. The introduction and dissemination of relativity were significant events in the Chinese history of modern physics.'

The Commercial Press played a significant role in this process.

Nine months in China saw some significant milestones passed in Russell's personal life. Initially, his Chinese hosts were somewhat bemused

In the foreground are Bertrand Russell, Edith Russell and Y. R. Chao, a Chinese-American scholar of distinction who nearly fifty years previously had acted as Russell's interpreter in China. (Date of photo: 1968)

by Dora Black's presence, but evidently accommodated the couple happily enough. During the early months of 1921, Dora became pregnant, which fulfilled Russell's long-held wish to become a father. In September, they married in London, shortly before John was born, days after Russell's divorce from his first wife, Alys Pearsall-Smith, came through.

Before he and Dora knew they were to be parents, Russell suffered a near-death experience. In March 1921, he contracted pneumonia after bathing in hot springs near Beijing and was close to death on several occasions during the weeks that followed. His life was saved by the great efforts of a young doctor at the German Hospital, Franz Esser, with Dora's help and the administration of some vital medication. Dr Esser renewed contact with Russell in 1956, by which time he had also been teaching philosophy in China, using Russell's *A History of Western Philosophy* as a textbook, though not in Chinese translation, it seems.

Commercial Press recently reprinted tens of thousands of copies of *A History of Western Philosophy*. It is recommended reading for high school and university students in China. They may not read all of it, but Russell has a growing following among the new generation of young adults, just as he has amongst their parents. 'What I have lived for' was the spontaneous response, when suggestions of memorable and accessible

Russell texts were sought from young publishers. This short text is to be published in *The World of English*, Commercial Press's monthly magazine for young people who want to improve their English. Written in longhand in July 1956, this was the prologue to Russell's *Autobiography.*

References

**The Selected Letters of Bertrand Russell, Volume 1, The Private Years, 1884-1914, Volume 2, The Public Years, 1914-1970*, edited by Nicholas Griffin, Routledge, 2001

** *The Practice and Theory of Bolshevism*, page x, Spokesman, 1995

*** *Modern China: A Very Short Introduction*, Rana Mitter, Oxford University Press, 2008

With grateful acknowledgements to Commercial Press in China and to Kenneth Blackwell and the Russell Archives at McMaster University, Canada, especially for their generous help with illustrations.

The Commercial Press began life as a printing company in Shanghai, in 1897. Five years later, in 1902, the Chinese scholar, Zhang Yuanji, joined with the founders of the printing press to set up an editorial and translation department, thus launching Commercial Press as China's first modern publishing house. Since then it has published more than 30,000 titles. In addition to translations, since its earliest days, Commercial Press has made a great contribution to documenting and developing Chinese culture. In 1954, Commercial Press moved to its current premises in the centre of Beijing, where it compiles and translates academic works in philosophy, politics, economics, history and geography, as well as dictionaries, reference books in Chinese and other languages, research works, textbooks, and popular books. Widely acknowledged as China's pioneering publisher, the high quality of its output endures as Commercial Press prepares for its 120th anniversary in 2017.

* * *

'In Shanghai we were taken to Commercial Press, an impressive publishing venture, which was bringing out translations into Chinese of modern books.' Dora Russell, The Tamarisk Tree

Russell's 'WHAT I HAVE LIVED FOR'

Three passions, simple but overwhelmingly strong, have governed my life: the longing for love, the search for knowledge, and unbearable pity for the suffering of mankind. These passions, like great winds, have blown me hither and thither, in a wayward course, over a deep ocean of anguish, reaching to the very verge of despair.

I have sought love, first, because it brings ecstasy – ecstasy so great that I would often have sacrificed all the rest of life for a few hours of this joy. I have sought it, next, because it relieves loneliness – that terrible loneliness in which one shivering consciousness looks over the rim of the world into the cold unfathomable lifeless abyss. I have sought it, finally, because in the union of love I have seen, in a mystic miniature, the prefiguring vision of the heaven that saints and poets have imagined. This is what I sought, and though it might seem too good for human life, this is what – at last – I have found.

With equal passion I have sought knowledge. I have wished to understand the hearts of men. I have wished to know why the stars shine. And I have tried to apprehend the Pythagorean power by which number holds sway above the flux. A little of this, but not much, I have achieved.

Love and knowledge, so far as they were possible, led upward toward the heavens. But always pity brought me back to earth. Echoes of cries of pain reverberate in my heart. Children in famine, victims tortured by oppressors, helpless old people a hated burden to their sons, and the whole world of loneliness, poverty, and pain make a mockery of what human life should be. I long to alleviate the evil, but I cannot, and I too suffer.

This has been my life. I have found it worth living, and would gladly live it again if the chance were offered me.

China's Road to Freedom

Bertrand Russell

Russell's farewell address was delivered at the Board of Education, Beijing, on 6 July 1921, and published the next day in The Peking Leader.

The foreigner who ventures to have an opinion on any Chinese question incurs a great risk of complete folly, particularly if, as in my case, his stay in the country has been short and his knowledge of the language is nil. China has an ancient and complex civilization, the most ancient now existing in the world. The traditions of China are quite different from those of Europe. China has in the past achieved great things in philosophy, in art and in music, but in all these respects, what has been done has been practically independent of European influence and widely different from all that issued out of the Hellenic culture. The mere effort to understand a society whose religion and morals have been framed in independence of Christianity requires for a European no small amount of psychological imagination. When one adds to all this the difficulty of ascertaining the facts concerning modern China, it is evident that any European is likely to go far astray in an attempt to lay down a programme of reform for the Chinese nation. For all these reasons, I am persuaded that those Chinese who have the welfare of their country at heart will have to frame their own programme and not rely too much upon the intellectual assistance of foreigners. Nevertheless, I am venturing to put before you some considerations as to the state of China and the way in which it might be improved – considerations which have grown up in me slowly during my stay among you and were by no means present to my mind when I first landed.

Two things of a very general nature seem to me evident: the first that it is not to be desired that China should adopt the civilization of Europe in its entirety; the second, that the traditional civilization of China is inadequate to present needs and must give way to something radically new.

The evils of European civilization have been made obvious to all thoughtful observers by the Great War and its outcome. In the early days of the war most Europeans imagined that these evils were not inherent in our system, but would be eradicated by the victory of one's own side, whichever that might be. This has proved to be a delusion. The basis of our civilization is capitalistic industrialism, a system, which, though in its early stages it brings about immensely rapid technical and material progress, cannot but lead on to increasingly destructive wars, first for markets and then for raw materials. It is by no means improbable that our Western civilization may go under in the course of these wars and of the class conflicts due to the opposition of capital and labour. Even if our civilization should survive, it is to be feared that it will become increasingly mechanical, with a constantly augmenting disregard for the individual and his idiosyncrasies. From such a civilization little that is of value is to be expected. It is, therefore, not by mere imitation of Western ways that the Chinese can do most for the welfare of their own country or of the world.

On the other hand, the traditional civilization of China based upon Confucianism tempered by Buddhism has worn itself out, and is no longer capable either of inspiring individual achievement or of solving the internal and external political problems with which China is beset. For the last thousand years or so this civilization has been decaying, slowly losing vigour as the Graeco-Roman civilization lost vigour in the centuries preceding the barbarian invasion. I think these evils are inseparable from an ancient tradition which is greatly respected, no matter what that tradition may be. It is necessary for each generation to think and feel for itself, and not to seek wisdom in the utterances of ancestors, however wise their ancestors may have been in their own time. I hear it said by Europeans that China would go to pieces morally if respect for the teaching of Confucius were lost. Perhaps this might be the case if a mere vacuum were left in the mental region from which that teaching had been removed, but it would most certainly not be the case if a newer doctrine, more suited to modern problems, could inspire the same belief and the same enthusiasm as must have been inspired by Confucianism in its creative period. The Chinese reformer, therefore, if I am not mistaken, will be no more willing to uphold what is traditional in his own country than to seek novelty by slavish imitation of the West. I am convinced that China, in the future as in the past, has a distinctive contribution to make to civilization, and something more than mere quantity to add to the world's mental possessions.

Passing from these generalizations to the actual state of your affairs, every reasonable man is convinced of the necessity of putting an end to the present condition of anarchic militarism. This is common ground among all reformers, from the mildest to the most extreme; but the method by which it is to be achieved is a matter of endless controversy. Among Europeans especially there is a tendency to favour restoration of the monarchy, but such a step can hardly be expected to appeal to the progressive Chinese. It is not by restoring old conditions that new problems can be solved.

It is clear, of course, that a radical and permanent solution must depend upon education. But education is a somewhat vague word, and any education worthy of the name is difficult to secure under the present political conditions, as the course of the teachers' strike has indicated. The education that China needs must be at once widespread and modern. It must not be, as in the past, the privilege of a favoured minority, nor the mere learning of ancient books and their commentators. It must be universal and must be scientific and the science must not be merely theoretical, but in close touch with modern industry and economics. So long as the bulk of your population is uneducated it will be incapable of supporting an industrial state or of resisting the ambitions of ruthless adventurers.

But the building up of such a system of education in a country such as yours is an immense task, requiring a generation for its fulfilment, even with all possible good will on the part of the government. You would not, to begin with, have the necessary supply of teachers, nor would the State be able to support the expense without a much greater development of industrialism than has hitherto taken place in China. And until you have a better government than you have now, you will not be able to secure even the preliminary measures. All that can be done at present in the way of education is to the good, and is, as the mathematicians say, necessary, but not sufficient. Thus the need for education brings us back to economic and political problems as its pre-conditions.

I think it must be taken as nearly certain that your industrial resources will lead in the near future to a great development of industrialism. I am by no means convinced that industrialism will be a boon to China, or can ever be anything but a misfortune to any country, but if, as I believe, industrial development is in any case inevitable, it is a mere waste of time to argue whether it is desirable or undesirable. The only problem of practical importance for you is the problem of developing industrialism with the minimum of attendant evils and the maximum of national and cultural advantage.

All the Great Powers are anxious to secure a share in the exploitation of your resources, and unless you develop more national strength than you have hitherto shown, you will be unable to withstand aggressions fomented by foreign industrialists.

I see that the American ex-Minister, Mr. Crane, has been advocating international control for China on the ground that the Chinese government cannot keep order, a prospect which grows not unnaturally out of the Consortium. There is much to be said for international control, not only in China but also in other countries. If England were subject to it, there would be an end to the reign of rapine and murder in Ireland. In America also Mr. Crane's proposal might be adopted with advantage. In that country there are constantly recurring Boxer risings – against the negroes. Under international control these rising might be put down by contingents of black troops drawn from all parts of Africa, and Fifth Avenue might be enlivened by memorial arches erected to the most prominent victims. International control of all nations must be the ultimate goal of all who wish to further the cessation of war which is only possible by substituting law for the present anarchy in relations between States. But international control, when it comes, must recognize the citizens of different states as equals, and not subject some of them to a despotism exerted by a league of certain others. No doubt the Chinese government is bad, but so are all other governments, and I doubt whether the Chinese government does as much harm as those of the Powers which were victors in the war. International control cannot, I am convinced, be a boon to China until the existence of a national State in China is fully assured, and until this state is strong enough to repel all attempts at exploitation by foreign capitalists backed by armies and warships.

I think the most urgent need of China is the development of active patriotism, especially among those who, by their education, are the natural teachers of public opinion. Japanese aggression has begun to produce a movement of this kind, but something much more active, instinctive, and widespread is necessary if China is to be saved from subjugation. Your Empire subsisted for thousands of years without coming into contact with any really formidable enemies. Even the Tartars and Manchus who acquired dominion were few and made a comparatively small mark upon Chinese civilization.

Consequently patriotism, which is chiefly evoked by the need of self-defence, plays little part in Chinese traditional morality. Its place was taken, more or less inadequately, by respect for the Emperor. And this substitute for patriotism has been destroyed since you became a Republic. Unfortunately you now for the first time in your history are faced with the danger of foreign aggression on the part of really formidable nations, and therefore the necessity of patriotism has become urgent. If your independence is to be preserved, it is necessary to transfer to the nation the kind of devotion which has hitherto been given to the family. The family is too narrow a group for modern needs, and a race which upholds the family as strongly as it is upheld in China, cannot develop that integrity and zeal in the public service without which no modern state can prosper.

It would of course be absurd to hope that public spirit could in a short time be diffused among the bulk of the population, but this is by no means necessary for the beginning of regeneration. Ten thousand resolute men, inspired by an ideal and willing to risk their lives, could acquire control of the government, regenerate Chinese institutions, and institute an industrial development which should be free from the evils associated with capitalism in the West. Such men would have to be honest, energetic and intelligent, incapable of corruption, unwearying in work, willing to assimilate whatever is good in the West, and yet not the slaves of mechanism like most Europeans and Americans. The powers of evil in China are not strong; they only seem so because the opposition to them is too theoretical.

There is one question which I find on the lips of almost all the thoughtful Chinese whom I have met and that is the question: 'How can we develop industry without at the same time developing capitalism and all its evils?' This is a very difficult question, and I do not know whether you will in fact succeed in solving it. When I first came to China I thought it insoluble, but I am now of the opinion that if you create such a band of resolute men as I have mentioned it would be possible to solve the problem. But it is useless in China to approach the economic problem directly; the political problem must be solved first. Until you have a strong and honest State, with able and incorruptible administration, you cannot institute any form of genuine socialism or communism. Suppose, for example, that your mines were now nominally nationalized; it is as clear as noon day that the profits to be derived from them would go to the Tuchuns [warlords] and their armies, not to the people. Political reform must precede any desirable economic development in China.

Political reform in China cannot for many years to come take the form of democracy after the Western model. Democracy presupposes a population that can read and write and that has some degree of knowledge as to political affairs. These conditions cannot be satisfied in China until at least a generation after the establishment of a government devoted to the public welfare. You will have to pass through a stage analogous to that of the dictatorship of the communist party in Russia, because it is only by some such means that the necessary education of the people can be carried through, and the non-capitalistic development of industry effected. The Russian Bolsheviks, as is natural to pioneers, have made many mistakes, more especially in the measures which antagonized the peasants. They are now, very wisely, repealing these measures, and those who follow them on the same road will be able to profit by their experience. When I was in Russia, I was much concerned with the Bolshevik attempt to introduce their methods and aims into Western countries. I believe this to be a quite useless attempt. Where there is already a developed industry and an educated proletariat, different methods must be adopted, and democracy must be preserved. But where, as in Russia and China, these conditions are absent, where there is a population which is neither educated nor accustomed to industrial processes, the methods adopted by the Russian communists seem, in broad outline, the best possible.

Various ways of organizing non-capitalistic industry have been suggested by various schools. There is anarchist communism, where, as in ancient Poland and in the League of Nations, no decision can be taken unless it is unanimous. There is syndicalism, which is a kind of federation of trade unions; there is State Socialism, which is the system adopted in Russia; and there is Guild Socialism, which is a blend of syndicalism and State Socialism. Anarchist communism, syndicalism, and Guild Socialism all presuppose a developed industry and the habits of industrialism. They are therefore impossible as the first step towards socialism in an undeveloped country. The early developments of industry must – so it seems to me – be either capitalistic or state-socialistic. Accordingly, if I am confronted by the problem: 'How can China develop her industries without capitalism?' I must reply: 'In the first instance only by State Socialism.' State Socialism has grave drawbacks, and in an undeveloped country reproduces many of the evils of capitalism. But I believe it is easier to pass from it to a better system, when industrial and educational progress makes it possible, than it is to eradicate capitalism when once it has acquired the hold it has in England and America.

There is much that is not essential in the practice of the Bolsheviks, and in non-essentials I do not desire to see them imitated. The essential thing is the State ownership and exploitation of mines, railways, waterways, and all urban and industrial land. (Theoretically, agricultural land should also belong to the State, but this raises such difficulties with the peasants that in a country of small proprietors it is not politically feasible on any large scale.) If this system is to avoid the inequalities of wealth which are among the evils of capitalism, the officials who direct industry must not use their power, as capitalists do, to extort vast fortunes out of the workers. This requires a degree of self-denial which can only be secured by a great enthusiasm and a great devotion to an ideal. Further, if the system of State Socialism is not to remain a bureaucratic tyranny, those who carry it out must be imbued with the love of democracy and liberty, and must direct their efforts to the realization of these as soon as the people can be sufficiently educated. It is mainly in this that I think the Russian communist party open to criticism: a system which gives all power to the communist party seems to its members quite satisfactory, and they are in no hurry to pave the way for a greater freedom and a wider distribution of power.

It is customary among communists to maintain that economic factors are the only ones of importance in the life of a community. This seems to me an entire delusion. I believe that ethical factors are at least as important. Consider the ethical qualities required of the men who are to bring about such an economic revolution in China as I have been suggesting. Such men, in the first place, will have to be intellectuals by training, but largely soldiers by profession. They will have to fight anarchic militarism within, and the whole might of capitalistic Powers without. What this means can be seen from what Russia has had to endure from the hostility of reactionary governments. In the course of the fighting, many will lose their lives, and all will have to endure hardships and the persecution of mankind. Assuming the victory won, the victors will be in a position to secure wealth and a long term of power for themselves; but they will have to forego wealth and prepare for the abolition of their power in favour of a more democratic system at the earliest possible moment. To pursue this course steadfastly to the end requires ethical qualities of the highest order. Especially rare is the willingness to abrogate power secured after a bitter struggle.

The great difficulty of the Bolshevik method of introducing Socialism lies in the severity of its ethical demands. The Russian Bolsheviks seem, on the whole, successful in resisting the temptation to wealth, but likely to succumb to the temptation to prolongation of their power. All their talk against democracy and in favour of the dictatorship of what they call the proletariat is, in essence, merely camouflage for their love of power. In China, so far as I have been able to observe the national character, one might expect the opposite failure, because the love of money seems to be stronger than the love of power. The love of money is, I think, the greatest danger you will have to combat if you attempt a non-capitalistic development of industry.

The ethical difficulties of the line of action I have been suggesting are so great that I cannot feel any confidence in its practicability. China is ruled at present by a set of Tuchuns whose dominant passion is money. You can only defeat them if you love the welfare of China more passionately and more energetically than they love money. This is a high standard, but what I have seen of Young China makes me not despair of its attainment.

If you cannot realize a moral and economic revolution, the alternative is a gradually increasing foreign control, perhaps leaving China's nominal sovereignty intact, but securing all real power to foreigners through possession of economic resources. Such a system would produce a growth of industrial capitalism, and the training of a population accustomed to industrial work – at first only in its lower grades, but later on probably in higher grades also. This process might lead after about a century to a movement for national liberation. But the movement would find success just as difficult then as now, and a century would have been wasted. Meanwhile the habits of capitalism would have been acquired, and would probably prevent the establishment of socialism even if national independence were achieved. From every point of view, therefore, a vigorous movement in the near future is infinitely preferable to the policy of drifting while foreign nations act.

Industry and the economic side of life have been thought of in the West too much as the ends of existence. They are not ends, but mere means to a good life. The ideal to be aimed at is a community where industry is the servant of man, not his master; where there is sufficiency and leisure for all; where economic aims are not dominant; where leisure is used for art and science and friendship, instead of being sacrificed to the production of an excess of commodities. China has many of the qualities required for realizing this ideal, particularly the artistic sense and the capacity for civilized enjoyment without which leisure has little value. These qualities make it possible to hope that China may lead the world in the next stage of development, and give back to the restless West something of that inner calm without which we must perish in frantic madness. In this way not only China, but the whole world, may be regenerated by your achievements.

Source: The Collected Papers of Bertrand Russell, Volume 15, Uncertain Paths to Freedom: Russia and China, 1919-22, edited by Richard A Rempel, Beryl Haslam, with the assistance of Andrew Bone, Albert C Lewis, Routledge 2000

Don't mention the children

'Israel bans radio advert listing names of children killed in Gaza.'
Guardian, *24 July 2014*

Don't mention the children.
Don't name the dead children.
The people must not know the names
of the dead children.
The names of the children must be hidden.
The children must be nameless.
The children must leave this world
having no names.
No one must know the names of
the dead children.
No one must say the names of the
dead children.
No one must even think that the children
have names.
People must understand that it would be dangerous
to know the names of the children.
The people must be protected from
knowing the names of the children.
The names of the children could spread
like wildfire.
The people would not be safe if they knew
the names of the children.
Don't name the dead children.
Don't remember the dead children.
Don't think of the dead children.
Don't say: 'dead children.'

Michael Rosen

From the new collection of the same title
www.smokestack-books.co.uk

THE
Week
A news analysis for socialists 9d.
JEREMY
CORBYN

Internationalist at work

Jeremy Corbyn

Written in 2011 as the Foreword to Spokesman's new edition of J. A. Hobson's influential classic, Imperialism: A Study, *the Leader of the Labour Party surveys a long history.*

J A Hobson wrote his great tome in a different age. His thoughts were dominated by the zenith of the British Empire and the Boer War. The outcome of the war demonstrated Britain's then ability in sustaining global reach, since Elizabethan times, but also its extreme vulnerability. At home the poor physique of working class soldiers led to Haldane's investigation into working class health and living conditions. The difficulty in containing the rebellious Boers, and the huge opposition to the war, encouraged further doubts about the whole Empire project.

What was remarkable was that Hobson wrote *Imperialism* at the end of the scramble for Africa in which Britain had gained enormous tracts of land, and Rhodes was busying himself with the Cape to Cairo railway project. The most cynical of western manoeuvres, the Congress of Berlin in 1884, had agreed on the lines on the map, which largely still exist and have been the cause of endless wars and the loss of many lives.

What is interesting is the way in which Hobson contrasts the 'new' African Empire and global reach that Britain had finally gained for itself with the two earlier editions of Britain's empire. The American Empire had collapsed in the eighteenth century, when the thirteen colonies rebelled and finally gained their independence; British efforts to re-take them were unsuccessful. Even despite the US Civil War, the new power over the water was now almost as great as the old imperial powers of France, Britain and Spain.

In effect, Hobson accepts that America had gone, and that the analysis should be looking at the dilemma between the 'real' British Empire in India and the new one in Africa and scattered islands across the oceans.

For someone who was revered by Marxists, and quoted by Lenin, for his analysis of the pressures to extend empire, his analysis of the then current Empire, and its future, was not very revolutionary. What is brilliant, and very controversial at the time, is his analysis of the pressures that were hard at work in pushing for a vast national effort in grabbing new outposts of Empire on distant islands and shores. His painstaking analysis of the costs, and the alleged benefits, of Empire is very powerful.

Pages of trade statistics show how the vast military spending on naval escorts, army postings and the human costs of wars had made little difference to Britain's trade in comparison to those countries who had little or no overseas places but successfully traded. The characterisation of the political and commercial interests that fed the cause of new empire is almost a parallel for our times. Then, as now, the popular press presented a general view of British superiority over the rest of the world, which effectively opened a space for the unholy alliance of an ambitious military high command and huge commercial interests. This created opportunities for arms manufacturers, business for shipping companies, and protected closed markets for British companies. It was also the mainstay of what had become traditional British industries such as cotton. Thousands of people were working in mills all across Lancashire and Yorkshire making products from raw materials which were imported over thousands of miles, and exported in reverse over the same routes.

What is attractive is Hobson's ability to separate and disassemble the interests of the commercial and imperial aims. He makes the valid point that other European countries, without the benefit of empires, manage to be successful trading and industrial powers in their own right.

Hobson's railing against the commercial interests that fuel the role of the popular press with tales of imperial might, that then lead on to racist caricatures of African and Asian peoples, was both correct and prescient. The way in which the British press portrayed Ghandi in the 1930s, or Kenyatta in the 1950s or, indeed, Argentina's soldiers and sailors in the 1980s shows the tricks have not changed dramatically.

The other relationship that has not changed at all is the link of these interests to the supposed national interest and the parroting of prejudices in Parliament. From John Bull and Cecil Rhodes in the nineteenth century, the khaki politicians who encouraged thousands to their deaths in 1914, and then the later colonial and imperial wars, the cynical manipulation has continued. Indeed, as with previous wars, there were deliberate media and political attempts to denigrate whole peoples in the run up to the wars in Iraq and Afghanistan.

Hobson's comments in Chapter V when he says that

> 'the increased hostility of foreign nations towards us in the last thirty years of the nineteenth century may be regarded as entirely due to the aggressive imperialism of those years …'

are a clear assertion of the real process that was taking place. This is followed by a table of costs that demonstrates how colonial trade rose from £184 millions in 1884 to £232 millions in 1903, but that arms costs went from £27 millions to £123 millions in 1902. This vast expenditure, a four-fold rise in eighteen years, (partly occasioned by the Boer War) encouraged the intensity of the growing arms race and colonial competition between Britain and Germany.

Hobson describes the way that the conglomeration of Army and Naval Officers, serving and retired, media opinion formers, and the whole retinue of manufacturers and arms dealers created a juggernaut that cost the nation, and ultimately, the world, dear.

In Chapter VII of his book Hobson develops a thesis that, to me, is strange, and at variance with the general analysis he presents against empire. He discusses the issues of organisation and activity of an empire and seems to be heading, in part, in the direction of some kind of Anglo Saxon Empire. This was long before the French idea of Overseas Departments and a global empire based on the cultural norms of the mother country. In this section Hobson makes some very prescient comments on the cultural identity and power of both India and China. Now emerging as the two most populous nations in the world and of ever increasing importance. In 1902, neither was united as a nation, both were wholly or partly occupied and controlled by European powers. His analysis was based on the obvious issues of population and resources, but also on the understanding of the colonial and technical traditions of both countries. China was clearly the most pre-eminent power for most of the past millennium and is now, in reality, returning to the technical pre-eminence it enjoyed before the European industrial revolutions.

What Hobson also observed was the growing industrial and imperial power of China; expansion and casting an eye towards the Pacific. In very prescient observations he saw military rivalry with the United States. Forty years later, a vicious conflict was in full swing between the USA and Japan in World War Two.

Reading Hobson's works now, at the end of the first decade of the twenty-first century, and acknowledging all that has happened in the huge sweep of imperial and post-colonial history, he deserves enormous credit and recognition. At his time of writing the British Empire was at its zenith, as were the French and German Empires. The European powers were feeling very pleased with themselves, having divided Africa amongst themselves at the Congress of Berlin in 1884. They also accepted the Monroe Doctrine, which gave the United States the whip hand over the former Spanish colonies of Latin America. US power, already huge, and its armed forces, soon to become more than a match for the Europeans, were honed from their domestic arms race in the Civil War. Active in aggression and occupation in Mexico, Cuba, the Philippines, their forces were ideally equipped for their initially reluctant participation in the Great War.

The Europeans, meanwhile, were concerning themselves with the challenge of the declining Ottoman Empire. National competition, huge leaps in arms technology, and nationalist rhetoric encouraged the descent into the abyss of the First World War. The millions who died in the trenches and mud of the Western Front laid down their lives for each other's empires. The whole allied edifice came crashing down when Russia withdrew, following the revolution, the Germans surrendered, and faced the arrogance of the victorious allies in Versailles.

The complexities of Versailles are often presented as the end of Empire but were, in fact, a change of gear and approach whilst preserving the colonial sensitivities of Britain and France. The German colonies were divided up between the victorious powers, while the Ottoman Empire was divided into the now notorious 'mandates'. Woodrow Wilson and his 'fourteen points' were the high point of articulation of then American liberal thinking, but tinged with more than a nod towards rapidly developing industrial and military US power.

Even as the great powers were humiliating Germany at Versailles and sharing out the spoils of war, they were united in detestation of the nascent Soviet Union. An alliance of all the victorious powers was equipping the Tsarist forces and fighting the Red Army. The Soviet Union survived, and expelled those forces as huge workers' risings were taking place in Europe, particularly in Germany.

The era of traditional empire was over, but was imperial thinking? Britain and France clung on to their colonial possessions with increasing difficulty and inability to pay for the rising military cost of subjecting people in revolt against the notion of distant European control of their lives. Both countries indulged in grand self-delusions of huge buildings such as Lutyens' palaces in New Delhi and attempts at uniting the empire with new shipping and airlines. Astonishingly, at a time of depression and rapid economic decline at home, Imperial Airways was presented as a step forward; there were massive Empire Day festivities and grand royal tours of the Empire.

The costs of World War Two and the loss of prestige of the European colonialists did not prevent Britain, France and The Netherlands attempting to re-take their 'possessions' in Asia from the Japanese and return to the 1930s. In the case of Vietnam and Indonesia, this was done with the enlisted support of surrendered and then conscripted Japanese soldiers.

Suspicion of Britain and France's role in their colonies temporarily fuelled American suspicions of a war to re-create empires. Britain was forced into independence of the Indian Subcontinent in 1947 and the catastrophic partition into India and Pakistan. France lost the battle of Dien Bien Phu in 1954, and was thus forced out of Indochina. Colonial wars followed but, by the end of the 1960s, European empires in the sense of colonial possessions were over.

Empires collapse from a combination of factors, principally the difficulty of governing and sustaining a regime at a distance, but also from opposition to the whole notion of empire at home. The two pre-eminent European colonial powers of the twentieth century, Britain and France, both had enormous confusions on the Left about empire. Both countries had been through political revolution, which was immediately followed by racial and political acts of contradiction to the supposed ethics of the new forces. Cromwell, having defeated the monarchist forces in the Civil War in 1648, invaded and occupied Ireland in unparalleled brutality and savagery. The uprising of black slaves in Haiti, in 1798, was brutally repressed by French forces sent by Napoleon in the name of Liberty, Equality and Fraternity.

In a sense, that confusion and contradiction remained with the British Left who supported Empire Free Trade and dominion status in the 1920s. Elements of the French Left initially supported the war against independence for Algeria in the 1950s.

In many ways the military disaster of the Suez adventure in 1956, when Britain and France tried to prevent Egypt from nationalising the Suez Canal, was the end of their empires. The United States and the Soviet Union became the big poles in the globe and, in their own ways, developed empires of ideology and economy.

Since World War Two, the big imperial force has been the United States on behalf of global capitalism and the biggest, mostly US-based corporations. The propaganda for this has presented itself as a voice for 'freedom' and carefully and consciously conflated it with market economics.

The 1949 Congress for Cultural Freedom in Amsterdam was the European opening to accompany the military re-occupation under the guise of NATO. Thus, the Cold War was followed by American media and cultural values, in an attempt to create an empire of the mind. The hard power of their weaponry, the malign influence of the CIA, and its creation of pliant and friendly governments, actively suppressed and subjugated peoples in the poorest counties of the world.

The influence of the Soviet Union around the world was huge, but tempered by an inadequate industrial base in comparison to the United States and the ruinously expensive arms race that hastened its decline, and eventual collapse in 1991. But the Soviet influence was always different, and its allies often acted quite independently. Cuba, desperately dependent on Soviet support for its survival in the 1960s through to the 1980s, developed a quite independent foreign policy and enormous respect and stature amongst the poorest people, particularly in Latin America.

What the Cubans and, in particular, Che Guevara were preaching in the 1960s has an even greater resonance today in the Left of Latin America. The popular socialist movements of Bolivia, Ecuador and Venezuela owe much to his vision. The Bolivarian alliance, with its economic and social justice requirements, represents a challenge and appeal that the traditional Monroe Doctrine of military power accompanied by global capital cannot match at all.

If the US has problems in Latin America, it has far greater problems in relation to Islam and its behaviour around the world. Like all empires, the excessive use of natural resources and huge costs of its military create the paradigms of decline and collapse. The US has, since the end of World War Two, sought access to markets and materials. Challenged by OPEC in the 1970s, it has desperately tried to control and hang on to influence in the Middle East. Some of this thinking led to the wars in Iraq in 1990 and 2003.

Bush and Blair's assertion of the War on Terror in 2001 had as much to do with economic interests as any notion of 'security'.

Afghanistan, the longest lasting US military involvement apart from Vietnam, is fuelled by notions of security and assertion of military power, but also of the huge unexploited mineral reserves. The irony of Afghanistan is that the unsuccessful attempts by the western counties to occupy and control will probably lead to Chinese mineral extraction to fuel their industries. It would bring a wry smile to Hobson, who long predicted the rise of China at the expense of the western powers.

The huge issues facing the world are of unprecedented shortages of raw materials, food and land coupled with enormous military expenditure and a huge gulf between the richest and poorest. A sixth of the world's population are permanently hungry, the same number again are politely described as 'food insecure', whilst the ominous issues of over development, water shortages and loss of ecology, and thus sustainability, mount up.

Free market capitalism cannot provide for everyone, or sustain the natural world. Its very imperative is of ever hastening exploitation of all resources including people, and it needs armies and weapons to secure those supplies. The political appeal, unchallenged in the 1990s, of this concept is fast fading by a combination of Islamic opposition and the radical popular movements of landless and poor peoples in many poor countries. Increasingly, these movements also have a resonance in the cities of the industrial countries as well.

All empires asserted themselves by technology. The Greek and Persian Empires by language and communications, the Romans by settlement, efficient armies and technology of agriculture and craft. The huge empires of China were technologically well in advance of any other for several centuries. Despite not having the use of the wheel, horses or steam power, the American empires of Aztec, Inca and Maya could dominate and control through advanced technology of building and communications, and, of course, disciplined forces.

The brutality of European expansion from the sixteenth century was based on superior weaponry and industry, and the waging of a permanent cultural war both at home and in the occupied lands. The racist stereotyping of peoples by the Europeans allowed the slave trade to develop and prosper. It enabled the most appalling degradation of subjected peoples to take place and pour untold wealth into pockets of the merchant classes in the cities of Britain and Europe.

Culture is an important part of empire, as is source of knowledge and understanding of history. All countries encourage a very nationalist form of history teaching, and from that stems racism and perverted feelings of superiority.

Technology cannot be monopolised any longer, nor communication really be brought under control. The whole world has realised the lack of emperors' clothes through Wikileaks; the honesty of the imperial masters in the global market place is now forever under scrutiny.

However, the wars and conflict are about poverty and hunger and the competition of the powerful for resources. Thus, big corporations, with the support of national governments, grab land in the poorest counties to supply food and fuel for the future. Desperately poor people in Kenya and Guatemala watch as land is fenced in and luscious genetically modified crops are produced and flown out to feed the well-fed on overnight flights.

Migrant flows of people in desperate search of work and life occur all over the world; at any one time there are probably 200 million people on the move in search of a sustainable life. These people, the most exploited, are the Fourth World who travel and hope and try and survive, but often die on roads and railway lines, in seas and in poverty.

Western countries in Europe and the United States are finding they do not really control their own economies, that the contradictions of global capital are bigger than they are. They also realise that none of the world's institutions can really control anything. The United Nations, long seen as a hope for peace and order, has such limited power and resources it can only proclaim, not control any situation.

The wars that are now being fought are of ideas and economic power. The free market model cannot sustain or succeed; the more collectivist approach of the Non-Aligned Movement, and assertion of the needs of the poorer countries of the world, does provide hope.

However, the denial of individual and collective rights, opportunities for women, and the increasing polarisation between rich and poor contain the seeds of conflicts to come. The writings of Arundhati Roy, as a voice for the voiceless and oppressed, are as prescient for the future as any.

Hobson proclaimed against the absurdity and inadequacy of empire. In this era we need sustainability and justice. Neither is possible in an ideology committed to aggrandisement of wealth. A century ago, Hobson analysed the motive force of Empire in an era of uniforms, deference and unnecessary respect for power and authority. That ideology has been replaced by an obsession with money and exploitation, and it is just as pernicious and equally dangerous for the future.

West Papua
Still no choice

Carmel Budiardjo

In 1973, Carmel Budiardjo founded TAPOL to promote human rights, peace and democracy in Indonesia; 'tapol' means political prisoner. Her untiring work in this field was acknowledged when she received the Right Livelihood Award.

When the Second World War in Europe and Asia came to an end, late in 1945, the country now known as Indonesia was a Dutch colony, the Dutch East Indies. Within months, Indonesia became an independent country. In the far east of the Indonesian archipelago was a territory, known then as West Irian (now West Papua), whose fate became a matter of international dispute involving the United Nations, a dispute that still has not been resolved.

At that time, the Dutch Government was in favour of self-determination for the Papuan people, but it came under heavy pressure from Washington whose main concern was to secure a world free of communism. The fear was that this dispute might benefit the Soviet Union, whose role in defeating fascism had been widely acknowledged as being crucial.

The dispute eventually led to the New York Agreement (15 August 1962) between the United States, the Netherlands and Indonesia. However, the Papuan people were not involved in these discussions. As the academic, John Saltford, writes in his book, *The United Nations and the Indonesian Takeover of West Papua (1963-1969): An Anatomy of Betrayal*:

> 'It was the Papuans who had most to lose from the settlement. They played no part in the negotiations, but they would be the ones who would have to live with the consequences.'

No choice

What is the dispute about? The New York Agreement gave the Papuan people the opportunity to participate in an Act of Free Choice to determine whether they wanted to be an independent state or to continue to be integrated in Indonesia. But as it turns out, the Act of Free Choice was no such thing. Indonesia, which was at the time ruled by President Suharto and his powerful military forces, made it clear that there would be no choice; that Papuans were ignorant, lazy and too primitive. Universal suffrage was not the way the Act would be implemented. The decision would be taken by eight assemblies, comprising 1,022 members, most of whom had been chosen by military commanders. Moreover, the decision would be adopted by consensus. This was how 'elections' were conducted in Indonesia during the Suharto regime. At the time, President Suharto was quoted as saying:

> 'Any vote against Indonesia would be regarded as treason.'

In January 1969, the British Embassy in Jakarta, Indonesia's capital, made it clear that it knew what would happen. It has been quoted as saying:

> 'Most independent observers are convinced that, given a free choice, the majority of the local inhabitants would not vote for continued incorporation in Indonesia ... But it is clear that they are going to be disillusioned when the Act of Free Choice leaves the territory, as it inevitably will, an integral part of Indonesia.'

Human rights abuses

Since then, the people of West Papua have suffered numerous violations of their human rights, their freedom of speech and of assembly. Over the years, tens of thousands of people have been killed or seriously wounded, simply for taking part in peaceful demonstrations, waving their own flag, The Morning Star. This flag, which was adopted at the First Papuan Congress in December 1991, is an important symbol of their determination to win freedom. This was also when they adopted the name 'West Papua' and their own national anthem.

Over the years, many Papuan activists have been arrested and sentenced to long terms of imprisonment simply for taking part in peaceful actions. When they are arrested for waving their Morning Star Flag, they face the charge of '*makar*' – treason. According to the Indonesian Criminal Code, anyone charged with *makar* faces a sentence of up to twenty years.

Although Indonesia is now regarded as being a democratic country, following more than three decades of Indonesian military rule [1965-1998], West Papua still suffers the presence of many thousands of heavily-armed troops who are primarily responsible for the human rights violations that continue to occur there. Soldiers are hardly ever arrested. They enjoy impunity for their crimes.

Over the years, the sufferings of the West Papuan people have rarely gained recognition around the world. However, in November 2004, troops from the military élite force, Kopassus, abducted and murdered the chairman of the Papuan Presidium Council, Theys Hiyo Eluay. He had been invited to attend a military event but this was clearly a trap. On his way home, his car was ambushed, he was strangled, and his body was found two days later a short distance away. His chauffeur, Masoka Aristotle, managed to escape and was able to phone his family and tell them about what happened but, since then, he has disappeared with nothing known to this day about his whereabouts or what happened to him. On this occasion, there were protests in many countries.

Papuan political prisoners

Today, Filep Karma, a fifty-eight year old former government employee, is one of West Papua's best known political prisoners. Amnesty International, Tapol, and other human rights organisations frequently highlight his case. Karma was first arrested in July 1998, after leading a pro-independence rally on the small island of Biak. Following a military clampdown, he was was sentenced to six-and-a-half years in prison. According to several human rights organisations, about two hundred people were arrested together with him, including scores of women and children, many of who were tortured and raped.

Following an appeal, Karma's sentence was reduced to two years. However, this did not weaken his resolve to continue to struggle for his people and their inalienable right to self-determination. In December 2004, he led a peaceful flag-raising demonstration. This time, he was sentenced to fifteen years and he is still in prison. In August 2015, he was offered release for clemency. He refused to accept this, insisting that to do so would mean acknowledging that he had committed a crime. The Fairfax Media agency quoted him as saying:

> 'My point is that Indonesia must realise that it must free me unconditionally, restore my good name. It should also free other political prisoners in Papua and elsewhere in Indonesia and stop chasing those who are on the wanted list for expressing their freedom of speech.'

These are the words of a man of high principle, a man who has dedicated so many years of his life to the struggle of his people.

Rich natural resources

West Papua contains within its territory a copper and gold mine that is believed to be the largest source of these minerals in the world. But the

Papuan people are not the ones who enjoy the benefits of this abundance. West Papua's copper and gold have been exploited since the early 1970s by a US multinational corporation, Freeport McMoran, according to a contract granted by Indonesia during the Suharto era. As has always been the case in matters of this nature, the Papuan people were not involved in the negotiations that led to this contract. With the exception of a small number of people living in the vicinity of the mine who receive a small percentage of the profits, the huge earnings enjoyed by the company go to Freeport and its shareholders, while the Government of Indonesia also receives a share of the profits.

But there is a clear alternative for the international community. We should raise our voices loud and clear in support of the West Papuan people.

www.tapol.org

A new report has been produced by a group of foreign church representatives who visited West Papua earlier in 2015 to celebrate the arrival of the Gospel in the territory 160 years ago. The Quaker-led visit was highly unusual as foreign people are, generally speaking, not allowed access to West Papua. The church representatives made the visit at the invitation of Reverend Dr Benny Giay, the Moderator of the Kingmi Church in West Papua who said that Church leaders in West Papua feel as if they are 'surrounded by violence' and 'cannot escape'. The visitors wrote:

> 'We hoped to help to break down Papuans' experience of international isolation. We travelled without a *Surat Jalan* (Letter of Travel) from the police and visited Biak, Jayapura, the Paniai highlands and Manokwari and witnessed the suffering of the people and experienced the repressive presence of the state security apparatus first hand.'

* * *

'Rev Dr Benny Giay was not being dramatic in his letter. Only a month before we travelled to West Papua, four young people, some of them in primary school, were shot dead by the Indonesian police in Paniai, in the remote highlands. One of the young people had been savagely beaten by the army the night before. He and his friends had been holding a vigil at a makeshift chapel when a car drove by without its lights on. One of the young people yelled at the driver to put his lights on. The car stopped, soldiers hopped out and proceeded to beat the boy. The next day, on 8 December 2014, the boy's friends went to protest the beating. When they arrived in town, they saw the car.

Angry, they started hitting the car. This is when the police opened fire with live ammunition, killing four. Despite calls by civil society for a thorough and independent investigation, no action has been taken … It now seems that this will be one more example in a five-decade list of cases of impunity. It did not take much dialogue to peel back the layer of fear amongst many of the people we spoke to.'

Telling, not selling

Paola Totaro

Filmmaker Wim Wenders and philosopher Mary Zournazi have spent a decade exploring the visual and moral language for peace. Their book, Inventing Peace: A dialogue on perception, *is published by I B Tauris (£14.99). Journalist Paola Totaro explored further.*

At first glance, they seem an odd couple: Mary Zournazi, the little-known University of New South Wales philosopher, and the renowned German filmmaker Wim Wenders. But it is she who has been able to fluidly place into historical and scholarly context his free-flow musings on peace, as he pans here and there, drawing on vignettes and scenes from life, art and cinema to illustrate and explain his thoughts.

Images of war are everywhere but most of us find it difficult to invoke a sensation of peace, let alone a symbol or ideal capable of stirring visceral response. The invisibility is not just an unsettling reality but a profound conundrum that has occupied Wenders and Zournazi for more than a decade. Collated in the book *Inventing Peace*, an intellectual collaboration in the form of a sprawling dialogue, the duo not only ruminate on their own ideas but draw on the artists, filmmakers and philosophers who inspired them to explore a new visual and moral language for peace.

> *'Horror has not only become a best-selling export article of Hollywood, it is now accepted as legitimate food for the eyes and mind.'* – *Wim Wenders*

Wenders and Zournazi are in London for an 'In Conversation' at the Institute of Contemporary Arts, an elegant building in the sweep of white-stucco-faced Georgian terraces just off The Mall and Trafalgar Square. It is Thursday night and the presence of the revered filmmaker – and the duo's interlocutor, the glamorous feminist writer and Sylvia Plath scholar, Professor Jacqueline Rose – means the event is a sellout. The building is rammed with people, the bar full, the café and bookshop buzzing. With the question-and-answer session over, the movie man and the philosopher work patiently through the long queue of people keen for autographs in newly bought books. One fellow has brought 20-plus Wenders film posters he has collected over two decades and the director, without a hint of annoyance, signs each one.

We were supposed to meet for a chat earlier in the day but Wenders' hotel baulked because they did not have a private room free: ironically, his superstar status in Europe (the trademark heavy glasses and shock of silver curls are eminently recognisable) allows him little peace in public. At the ICA, a lissome, black-clad event manager whisks us to a quiet room upstairs, away from the crowd.

Seated in high-backed chairs, bottles of still water in hand, the two could not be more different interviewees. Wenders is quiet, contemplative and exudes a kind of benign patience and sense of duty. Zournazi, despite fighting a cold, is radiating excitement.

She says they met, pretty much by accident, on the eve of the Second Gulf War in 2003, not long after she had published a book examining perceptions of hope. It was a time when much of the world had divided itself along the axis of good versus evil and Zournazi was invited to give a talk in Sydney. She remembers a palpable hostility from the audience, which dismissed her questioning of the inevitability of conflict.

'A moral sensibility and vocabulary of what peace might mean were absent from the public debate just as much as they have been largely absent from history ... people thought I was deluded even thinking about peace,' she remembers.

Struck by the realisation that even public discourse mimics the structure of a battlefield, Zournazi became convinced then that her next project must be an examination of peace.

> 'I was looking for some way to kickstart the project and it came ... Wim was visiting Sydney and I heard him on radio. Nobody else was addressing alternatives to war; he was the only one talking about peace.'

Wenders says the 'moment' for him was during a visit to New York not long after the attack on the twin towers – his contemplative and brutally beautiful photo of Ground Zero still smoking is in the book (see p.52). He vividly describes entering a church to find people of many different faiths in one place, praying together.

> 'After 9/11 in New York there was a short time when I believed the utopian possibility that something so terrible could lead to something fantastic for

> mankind …' he says quietly. 'After 9/11 there was that pause. And then it was all wiped out by Afghanistan and Iraq.'

Wenders is adamant that *Inventing Peace* is not a political work. 'It is even hard to talk about the book. It is immersive, experiential, a transformative process, internally and in the imagination. It is a form of creativity … to try and find out why peace is so invisible,' he says.

He is convinced we are living through a period of existential confusion in which the response to real conflict and war expresses itself in a 'need [for] entertainment more gory than ever before'.

> 'We now accept horror as part of the human condition. It has not only become a best-selling export article of Hollywood, but consumers all over the planet have accepted it as legitimate food for the eyes and mind.'

This is a plague not restricted to the Western world. Shooting a short film in the Democratic Republic of Congo on violence against women for *Médecins Sans Frontières*, Wenders recalls being struck by the absence of men and boys in the village. He and his crew decided to explore and found them – old, young and very young men – crowded into a hut watching war movies on an old video player powered by a generator. His powerful four-minute short, *War in Peace*, is a moving testament to the addictive and deadening effect of immersion in both real – and cinematic – violence. This is one of two short films that can be downloaded with a code published in their book.

Wenders' profound sadness at this state of affairs is tangible and yet *Inventing Peace* manages to be an uplifting and inspiring book. Zournazi says they are indebted to the work of Martin Buber, the Austrian-born, Israeli Jewish philosopher best known for his philosophy of dialogue, a form of existentialism described in detail in his 1923 book *I and Thou*. Buber's belief – that the meaningfulness of human life is found in relationships – is a driving narrative in their writing. Equally important to them is the quantum physicist David Bohm's idea of dialogue as 'the artful process and flow between people that offers potential for change'.

Unique writing

Inventing Peace is a million miles away from the usual impenetrable academic tome, and its structure allows you to dip in and out. Nonlinear, it is an extended meditation, a kind of email to-ing and fro-ing (Zournazi calls it a 'dia-flow') which was honed into book shape during periods of intense face-to-face writing conducted in remote spots, including a cabin in the Mojave Desert.

Wenders extends the debate to the reader, asking he or she to 'think along, enter the dialogue'. His unique writing style is printed in the book exactly as he typed it, thus:

> I am not a philosopher,
> not even an intellectual,
> and I'm certainly not trying to sound like either:
> My writing style (which you see here for the first
> time in our book)
> does not pretend to look like poetry,
> or even try to evoke, let alone imitate it.
> It is simply my reflexive style of writing
> It helps me structure my thoughts,
> and as I am rather a filmmaker and photographer,
> therefore some sort of 'thinker in imagery',
> writing like this helps me 'see my thoughts'.

The result is indeed visual, as Wenders swoops and flows into the work of the plethora of artists who elate him. Among them are Charlie Chaplin, Michelangelo Antonioni, Akira Kurosawa and Robert Bresson, but most important to him (and the most joyous reading for us) are his observations on the *oeuvre* of the Japanese cinematographer Yasujirō Ozu, whose unstinting gaze on the stories of family unearth the moving and tender universality of human experience.

Wenders says Ozu belongs to what he describes as 'a lost paradise of filmmaking' and describes in detail the director's unique cinematic techniques – 50mm lenses, camera angles kept at the eye level of someone sitting on a tatami floor, dialogues between protagonists but delivered entirely to camera. All these, he says, reduce the distance between actor and viewer, creating a sense of respect in observation, a modest gaze devoid of judgement.

> 'Ozu taught ways of seeing the "other" in a different way. His is a loving, gentle gaze,' he says.

Described with a similar passion is the work of Andrew Wyeth, the great 20th century American painter known for his genial ability to distil tiny, ordinary moments in life and imbue them with a sense of wonder.

Wenders is not, however, bound by an atavistic view of the world. He writes with enthusiasm about the potential for 3D technology as an artistic vehicle for cinematic exploration of relationships and the

Wim Wenders

Ground Zero, New York, 8 November 2001

interconnectedness of humanity, and the making of his 2011 Oscar-nominated work on the German choreographer Pina Bausch, which was shot in 3D.

This exploration of artists that 'see' in a peaceful way led Wenders and Zournazi to the next step – which is to question the ethical consequences of what we are all guilty of doing and what they call 'looking and not seeing'. The duo muses that while the war-movie genre is now ubiquitous, no such peace equivalent exists. This void creates an ever more powerful and immersive viewing experience that simultaneously allows audiences to remain distant from indifference and cruelty.

Wenders says that in his own work he tries to find a language that reflects a world defined not by violence but human relationships. As an example he cites *Wings of Desire*, the acclaimed tale of angels in a pre-unification Berlin, and the post-Iraq war *Land of Plenty*.

> 'Film is a powerful medium. It is not just stories, it is a language between images that means that you work out in your own life what is between the lines. The subtext can be healing, friendly, or it can be the opposite, confuse or anger you. Every film teaches you a way of seeing.'
>
> 'It is a school of perception, even if it doesn't intend to be. It conditions you and this conditioning [to violence] is one of the things we look at.'

The right to space

The notion of space is a fundamental ingredient in both Wenders' and Zournazi's notions of peace, explored through the connections created by – and between – people. In film, allowing the watcher to see what the other is seeing provides a gentle push to take into account and perhaps even momentarily assume the point of view of the other person.

Wenders believes that the true acknowledgement of another's existential space negates the potential for conflict. 'As soon as you consider someone's space and you see that space around him or her, you have in a way eliminated the possibilities of war or violence, because respecting someone's space almost pulls the carpet out from under any violent act.'

I suggest to both authors that there is a striking absence of opinion or judgement in the book. After an uncomfortably long silence, Wenders says: 'An opinion is a violent act very often. An opinion is superimposed and very often neglects or denies the space or the right to a space that person has. You have an opinion of someone because he is a foreigner or belongs to that group or that group and immediately that person's void of their own space. It obliterates them.'

Zournazi laughs with gusto and says that Wenders' statement 'should be broadcast all over Australia!' For her, the book's publication comes at a particularly poignant time, as Australia struggles with asylum-seeker policies. 'Maybe we should be asking people to consider their ethical relationship with other people,' she suggests. 'It sounds trite and it is not meant to be. But what we all share is our humanity and there is something very special about that. It gets ignored in political discussion: we forget people are suffering and even if connections between people are small, it is those small connections that make the big things change.'

As we prepare to leave – Wenders is keen to join an old colleague for a drink downstairs – I ask him if I'm right to read a subtext of apology, and perhaps even melancholy, about the film industry, his industry, in the book.

The silence is momentarily terrifying but suddenly his hands, clasped quietly in his lap throughout the evening, come to life and the volume of his voice rises perceptibly.

> 'My industry is basically devoid of any ethics,' he says. 'I'm afraid to say that this was once part of filmmaking, that it was considered an ethical process. But basically today it does not include that anymore.'
> 'And, yes, there is a melancholy. Yes there is, because in the time I have lived cinema, most cinema turned from a way of expression to a product. And a product, as such, needs to be sold, whereas an expression needs to be told. Cinema is not about telling anymore, it is about selling.'

With grateful acknowledgements to the author for her kind permission to reprint and to The Saturday Paper in Australia, where this article first appeared.

www.paolatotaro.com
www.thesaturdaypaper.com.au

Wim Wenders and Mary Zournazi

Shakespeare and Tolstoy on Peace and War

John Gittings

John Gittings is the author of The Glorious Art of Peace *(OUP 2012, see* Spokesman 118*). This is an edited version of a talk given in June 2015 at Shipton-under-Wychwood Literary Festival.*

As we remember the First World War – and shall continue to remember it for the next four years – I shall take as my starting point for this enquiry into 'Shakespeare and Tolstoy on peace and war' a poem by Thomas Hardy, written at the end of the First World War, which poses the central question. It is a question which both Shakespeare and Tolstoy in different ways sought to address and to answer.

Thomas Hardy should be numbered more frequently among the so-called 'war poets' of the First World War (we should really call them 'peace poets'). He was much older than those whose names we usually remember, Owen, Blunden, Sassoon and others, and unlike them he had no direct experience of this war. But ever since the Boer War, over a decade earlier, he had in a number of poems expressed his anguish on the subject.

And in November 1918, he wrote a powerful and moving poem which was called, simply, 'On the Signing of the Armistice'. It concludes with this stanza:

Calm fell. From Heaven distilled a clemency;
There was peace on earth, and silence in the sky;
Some could, some could not, shake off misery:
The Sinister Spirit sneered: 'It had to be!'
And again the Spirit of Pity whispered, 'Why?'

Hardy had referred more than once in early writings to the 'Sinister Spirit' and to the 'Spirit of Pity' (most notably in his epic play *The Dynasts*) and he took the side naturally of the Spirit of Pity, and of the question which that spirit asked: Why? Why War?

Asking this question takes us beyond the position of being for or against war in general, or for or against a particular war, It makes us consider what are the driving forces behind war, and what are the means by which we can instead make peace or keep peace. It is a question which deeply concerned the early Christian fathers: for did not Jesus, they asked, say to Peter in the Garden of Gethsemane 'Put up your sword?' And we may remember the great saying of St Augustine, that

it is a higher glory still to stay war itself with a word, than to slay men with the sword, and to procure or maintain peace by peace, not by war.

The question 'why war' was one which pre-occupied the humanists of the Renaissance, the philosophers of the Enlightenment, and poets, novelists and peace thinkers of the modern age from the early 19th century onwards. And it is a question which lies at the heart of the approach of any great writer or thinker to the intellectual and moral challenge of peace and war.

War is one of the most significant nouns to appear in the texts of Shakespeare, as we can establish these days by carrying out a computerised word count. Foreign wars and civil conflict are central themes in the two sets of historical plays (*Richard II, 1 and 2 Henry IV, Henry V; and 1-3 Henry VI, Richard III*). The story of *Troilus and Cressida* is set during the most famous war in literature, the Trojan War. Acts of war bring the plots of *Julius Caesar*, *Macbeth*, *Timon of Athens*, and *Coriolanus* to their dramatic conclusions.

And yet the adjectives which Shakespeare uses to categorise war are almost always negative and pejorative. War is 'all-abhorred' (*1 Henry IV*) and 'cruel' (*Troilus* and *Coriolanus*), it is 'none-sparing' (*All's Well*) and 'mortal-staring' (*Richard III*), it is 'dreadful' (*3 Henry VI*), 'fierce and bloody' (*King John*), 'mad-brained' (*Timon*), and 'hungry' for men's blood (*Richard III*); it is a 'hideous god' which has a 'harsh and boist'rous tongue' (*2 Henry IV*).

Some who write approvingly of the phenomenon of war cite Skakespeare's phrase 'glorious war' as if it implies approval – perhaps he even coined the term? Indeed, the complete line which contains this phrase is one of the most famous in Shakespeare: it is the line which speaks of the 'pride, pomp and circumstance of glorious war!'. When Edward Elgar was looking for a title for his first two *Military Marches* (written by the way immediately after the Boer War in 1902), he chose the phrase 'Pomp and Circumstance' from this speech, but it is hardly an appropriate choice.

Context is all-important here. Let us reflect a little on this speech by Othello, for it is he who delivers the vivid word-picture painted by Shakespeare here of 'glorious war'. It comes at the tragic turning point of the plot of *Othello*, when the Moor has been convinced (falsely) by his lieutenant Iago that he is being betrayed by his wife Desdemona

> *I had been happy,* [he tells Iago] *if the general camp,*
> *Pioneers and all, had tasted her sweet body,*
> *So I had nothing known. O, now, for ever*
> *Farewell the tranquil mind! farewell content!*
> *Farewell the plumed troop, and the big wars,*
> *That make ambition virtue! O, farewell!*
> *Farewell the neighing steed, and the shrill trump,*
> *The spirit-stirring drum, the ear-piercing fife,*
> *The royal banner, and all quality,*
> *Pride, pomp and circumstance of glorious war!*

This is hardly an untroubled hymn to war, but the desperate cry of a man whose mind is already gripped by delusion – he even imagines that Desdemona might be capable of sleeping with his entire army. The lofty images of war in this speech should be seen rather as a flight of nostalgia for the supposed simplicities of martial life which may be no more real than the phantoms bred by Othello's jealousy. And this bitterly ironical passage is the only time that Shakespeare speaks of 'glorious war'.

Let us look at another passage from Shakespeare which is sometimes quoted to support the argument that human beings are, for better or for worse, attracted by war and over the ages have found war to be more exciting than peace. It comes from a scene in *Coriolanus* where the servants of the Volscian leader Tullus Aufidius have just learned that Coriolanus, the Roman war hero, has defected to their side, and they now look forward to Coriolanus joining in a war of revenge against his own people.

> *Why, then* (says one of them*), we shall have a stirring world again. This peace is nothing, but to rust iron, increase tailors, and breed ballad-makers.*

And the other servant replies: *Let me have war, say I; it exceeds peace as far as day does night; it's spritely, waking, audible, and full of vent. Peace is a very apoplexy, lethargy; mulled, deaf, sleepy, insensible; a getter of more bastard children than war's a destroyer of men.*

The irony and cynicism here is unmistakeable: it amounts to a parody of the arguments of those who argued in the Elizabethan age that you need a good war to toughen people up – for there was a strong war party in the court of Queen Elizabeth.

This is not to suggest that Shakespeare's views can be simply characterised as anti-war rather than pro-war. Even leaving aside the tricky question of how we can ascertain Shakespeare's own views when they are always expressed through the voices of his characters … However we should understand that for Shakespeare war and peace are always complex, not simple, issues, that in many cases the problem is handled with irony and ambiguity and, more often than not, that the argument comes down on the side of peace and against war.

The complexity of Shakespeare's vision may be gauged in a fascinating, but quite difficult, passage in Hamlet's last soliloquy, the moment in Act 4 when he stops hesitating and finally decides to take revenge on King Claudius for having murdered Hamlet's father. Hamlet has just watched a contingent of Norwegian troops march by – they had requested permission to cross Danish territory in order to invade Sweden – and he has asked a captain in the Norwegian army to explain what is the cause for which they will be fighting the Swedes. The Captain tells Hamlet that Norway and Sweden are in dispute over what he calls 'a little patch of land' which is hardly worth being farmed. It has, says the Captain, 'no profit in it but the name'. A classic territorial dispute, in other words, over something of no importance at all.

Hamlet replies to the Norwegian captain that

Two thousand souls and twenty thousand ducats
Will not debate the question of this straw:

His meaning is that the military engagement is likely to cost two thousand lives, and a large sum of money, all for an argument over a territorial trifle – a 'straw'. And in the soliloquy that follows, he reflects that not two thousand but twenty thousand soldiers may

… for a fantasy and trick of fame,
Go to their graves like beds, fight for a plot
Whereon the numbers cannot try the cause,

But then Hamlet, who only a moment ago has regarded the dispute as senseless and a waste of human life, switches his view. He now sees it as reflecting a sense of honour which obliges the Norwegians to fight for this territory however worthless it may be. And if honour does not allow them to stand by even though the cause be so trivial, argues Hamlet, how can he stand by and do nothing when his father has been killed and his mother has been taken into the bed of the killer? So he finally makes his mind up:

> *O, from this time forth,* (he concludes)
> *My thoughts be bloody, or be nothing worth*!

And the scene is set for the final act of blood and destruction, when Hamlet, his mother and his uncle all end up as corpses. Hamlet's argument which leads to this mayhem is, as one modern critic, Alex Newell, has pointed out, confused and irrational. For first he laments the loss of life which will occur when the Norwegian and Swedish troops fight over a scrap of land, but then he praises the sense of honour which drives them towards their slaughter (*The Soliloquies in Hamlet*, 1991, p. 77). But by doing so Shakespeare tells us a good deal both about Hamlet's confused state of mind and about the irrationality of violence and revenge.

We come now, as we must, to the consideration of *Henry V,* surely the one play of Shakespeare's which does beyond doubt celebrate martial patriotism and 'glorious war'. And it is true that the play has often been seen this way. In particular, King Henry's tribute to 'we happy few, we band of brothers' before the Battle of Agincourt has become part of the mythology of war in its most heroic, patriotic, and self-sacrificial guise. and it has continued to be invoked in recent times of British war, such as the Gulf War and the Iraq War.

This uncomplicated view of *Henry V* was questioned long ago by the essayist William Hazlitt, in his study of Shakespeare's characters published in 1817. Hazlitt wrote that the king 'seemed to have no idea of any rule of right or wrong, but brute force …' and that because Henry's own title to the English crown was doubtful, 'he laid claim to [the crown] of France'. Henry is an appealing character, Hazlitt acknowledged, but it is the appeal of 'a panther or a young lion in their cages in the Tower'. The controversy over how to interpret *Henry V* has continued ever since, and it may be illustrated here with one striking episode from the play.

Not long ago the Shakespearean scholars John Sutherland and Cedric Watts published an essay with this deliberately provocative title: '[Was] Henry V [a] war criminal' (*Henry V, War Criminal, and Other Shakespearian Puzzle*, 2000). Sutherland's question was provoked by a particularly problematic episode in the play during its portrayal of the Battle of Agincourt (the 600th anniversary of this battle is also being remembered in this year of 2015). Briefly, when the fight at Agincourt is almost won, Henry comes on stage with his escort and, according to the original stage directions, 'with prisoners'. Seeing that the French have brought up new reinforcements, he gives the order to prepare for further battle by first killing the prisoners. Here is the text from the quarto edition of *Henry V*:

Act 4, Scene 6 [Alarum]

King Henry V*: But, hark! what new alarum is this same?*
The French have reinforced their scatter'd men:
Then every soldier kill his prisoners:
[The soldiers kill their prisoners]
Give the word through.

Pistol: *Coup' la gorge.*

Pistol's remark in doggerel French makes the intention brutally clear. The editor of the Oxford Shakespeare text suggests that Pistol, who had his own prisoner in tow, may have performed this action on stage (Gary Taylor, ed., *Henry* V, pp. 65-6).

Now here is a rather remarkable fact. Neither Lawrence Olivier in his famous wartime film (1944) nor Kenneth Branagh in his more recent and much-praised version (1989) included this scene at all. Of course the killing of prisoners happens quite often in war, yet to show it on screen would have jarred with the heroic image of Henry, the noble warrior king.

Henry V was followed soon after by *Troilus and Cressida*, a play which throughout takes a jaundiced and cynical view of the virtues of war. From now on, Shakespeare's treatment of war becomes increasingly critical: his martial tragedies of the later period (*Othello, Macbeth, Antony and Cleopatra, and Coriolanus*) all have as their subject a general of great military prowess whose character is fatally flawed – by jealousy, ambition, sexual weakness, or pride.

Finally we may note that Shakespeare's last three plays all reflect a more mellow mood of peace. Peace is the last word of *Cymbeline*, *The Tempest* ends with the peaceful resolution of life's storms, and peace is the subject of the last speech of *Henry VIII* which looks forward to the mainly peaceful reign of Queen Elizabeth.

In her days every man shall eat in safety,
Under his own vine, what he plants; and sing
The merry songs of peace to all his neighbours:
God shall be truly known; and those about her

From her shall read the perfect ways of honour,
And by those claim their greatness, not by blood.

Let us move now from Shakespeare to Tolstoy, even if it seems over-ambitious to attempt to tackle these two great writers at the same time. They both present huge challenges to us. Shakespeare presents one kind of challenge to anyone who seeks to find out what Shakespeare thought on any particular issue, in this case the issue of peace and war. For Shakespeare does not speak directly to us but through his characters, he does not editorialise except occasionally in a few lines of prologue or epilogue. But if we know too little about Shakespeare as Shakespeare, one might say that we know too much about Tolstoy as Tolstoy. As well as his own autobiographical works, his novels contain fictionalised versions of himself – Pierre in *War and Peace*, Levin in *Anna Karenina*. We have his diaries, his wife's diaries, the memories of his children, of his friends and his enemies, the reports of the Tzarist secret police. We know what he was reading and his own critical views of what he read. We can follow the progression of his philosophy and idea, not to mention his personal weaknesses and obsessions over a period of some 60 years, almost thought by thought.

However we may simplify our approach on this occasion by concentrating on a very small portion of Tolstoy's life and thought – a portion of great importance but one that is often overlooked. Let us put to one side the last 30 years of his life when he embarked on his voyage of religious discovery and developed his ideas of what we now know as Tolstoyan pacifism. We may also leave a full analysis of *War and Peace* for another time. Let us instead concentrate upon Tolstoy's very early experience of war in real life, the actual business of killing or being killed, as refracted in the early writings in which Tolstoy reflects this experience, an experience which stayed with him for the rest of his days.

Tolstoy was still a comparatively young man, at the age of 34, when he settled down on his country estate in 1862, with his new wife Sonya, happier than he had been ever before, to start work on the novel which would become, over the next five or six years, *War and Peace*. So where did the wealth of descriptive and generally accurate description of the mechanics of war, and the horrors of war, come from? More important, from where did he derive the psychologically acute and vivid portrayal of the complex emotions which beset all those engaged in war, and most important of all, of the moral complexity presented by war to all those who are willing to think about it?

Ten years earlier, in 1852, disgusted with his spendthrift and idle life as a young man in fashionable Moscow society, Tolstoy had joined his brother who was an officer in the Tsarist army in the Caucasus – the region now known as Chechnya and Dagestan. The army was engaged in trying to subdue by force the local people, the Tartars, some of whom collaborated with their occupiers while the majority fiercely resisted. Tolstoy was described as a 'volunteer' when he arrived there but he was really what we would now call a 'war tourist', an observer and onlooker. However he soon applied for and eventually obtained a regular appointment as an artillery officer.

Tolstoy's diary for this period tells us that he was still struggling to improve his behaviour, without much success. He continued to gamble, this time with the army officers – he even had to sell the family home to meet his debts – and he continued to chase women, this time the local Tartar women. Tolstoy then and for the rest of his life was someone of many contradictions. But suddenly, in a diary entry of 6 January 1853, we find this short but revealing comment:

> *A stupid parade. Everyone drinks – especially my brother – and it's very unpleasant for me. War is such an unjust and evil thing that those who wage it try to stifle the voice of conscience within them. Am I doing right? Oh God, teach me and forgive me if I'm doing wrong.*

From the very beginning, Tolstoy was asking himself that great question posed by Thomas Hardy: Why? Why war? And Tolstoy posed it explicitly in his very first short story – only the second piece of his to be published. The story is called *The Raid*, and it is based upon his own experience of taking part in a punitive expedition launched against a hostile Tartar village. The village is burnt to the ground, but the army then has to retreat while being harassed by Tartar guerrillas, and suffers several casualties. This short story was published in a Moscow journal a year later, but with a number of cuts, most of which were imposed by the Russian censor. In the story, and especially in the material that was cut, we can see the beginning of Tolstoy's lifelong enquiry into the morality of war. Tolstoy begins with this bald statement:

> *War always interested me, not war in the sense of manoeuvres devised by great generals ... but the reality of war, the actual killing.* [How was it possible, he asked himself, for a soldier] *with no apparent advantage to himself, [to] decide to subject himself to danger and, what is more surprising still, to kill his fellow-men?*

Halfway through the short story, in a passage which also was cut by the censor, we find this already mature reflection.

> *War! What an incomprehensible phenomenon! When one's reason asks: 'Is it just, is it necessary?' an inner voice always replies 'No'. Only the persistence of this unnatural occurrence makes it seem natural, and a feeling of self-preservation makes it seem just.*

The passage continues with a long reflection on how the justice of the Russian campaign against the Tartar tribes is balanced – we might say cancelled out – by the justice of those desperate tribesmen and their families who fear the destruction of their villages and who take up arms to resist. In another passage, also deleted by the censor, Tolstoy describes vividly how the general in charge of the Russian troops allows them to loot and burn the village which they have captured.

Two years later Tolstoy, having by now joined the army, applied for a transfer from the Caucasus to the Crimean front. He saw action as an artillery officer there spending some time in one of the bastions of the Russian defence against the British, French and Turks. But he continued to write, and completed three pieces of reportage. The first, published in a Moscow magazine, was fairly straightforward and was commented on favourably by Tsar Alexander II; but passages in his second and third instalments describing the blood and carnage of the siege were suppressed by the Russian censor as 'anti-patriotic'. Here too we find themes which will appear in *War and Peace*, notably, the way in which a soldier can feel himself to be invincibly brave at one moment, yet succumb to abject terror and fear the next … the rapidity with which a peaceful scene with soldiers standing around and laughing and joking can turn into bloody carnage and severed limbs when a shell arrives in their midst, … the tendency for those who have survived a battle to dramatise and embellish their own memories of how they behaved during it. All these acute observations, which illustrate both the horrors of war and the human capacity for self-deception about war, can be found in Tolstoy's three Sevastopol sketches from the Crimean War. (These sketches, as well as *The Raid*, are included in the volume published as *Tales of Army Life*).

When Tolstoy started to write *War and Peace* ten years after the Crimean War he had not yet reached the conclusion that it was a human obligation to resist war and not take part in it. But his exceptional sensitivity to the ambiguities of human behaviour still enabled him to convey in *War and Peace* the moral complexity of war, its fatal fascination, and its unmitigated horror – the one sometimes following the other with terrible speed. This is powerfully conveyed in his description of the Russian troops at Austerlitz, fleeing in disorder and panic from the French across a narrow wooden bridge.

> *It was growing dusk. On the narrow Augesd dam where for so many years the old miller had been accustomed to sit in his tasselled cap peacefully angling, while his grandson, with shirt-sleeves rolled up, handled the floundering silvery fish in the watering-can ... – on that narrow dam amid the wagons and the cannon, under the horses' hooves and between the wagon wheels, men disfigured by fear of death now crowded together, crushing one another, dying, stepping over the dying and killing one another, only to move on a few steps and be killed themselves in the same way.*

Passages such as these may lead readers to conclude that Tolstoy already goes well beyond a sympathetic portrayal of human emotion, and of the haphazard way in which war unfolds, to convey an implicit judgement on war as such. Not all Tolstoyan scholars would agree, but the pioneering translator and friend of Tolstoy, Aylmer Maude (who with his wife Louise produced the translations of Tolstoy published by OUP which are still standard), had no doubt that *War and Peace* amounted to a condemnation of war. Certainly, it would take Tolstoy two more decades to reach the position that a true reading of Christianity requires one to reject violence in all its forms. However, in *War and Peace* Tolstoy had already moved a long way towards his later conviction that war is based upon a confidence trick: that wars are started by individuals with pretensions to exercise power, but that the reality of such power is a fraud.

Tolstoy set out his views on the nature of this power in the second epilogue *to War and Peace,* which like the other epilogues is often mistakenly regarded as wordy and superfluous to the book. Wars may appear to be justified by rational argument and decision, writes Tolstoy, but this is an illusion: These justifications release those who produce the events from moral responsibility; they are

> *like the broom fixed in front of a locomotive to clear the snow from the rails in front: they clear men's moral responsibilities from their path. Without such justifications, there would be no reply to the simplest question that presents itself when examining each historical event. How is it that millions of men commit collective crimes – make war, commit murder, and so on?*

Again, Tolstoy is asking that same question, the question with which we started: Why? Why War? Why not Peace?

We may conclude with this reflection: Shakespeare as well as Tolstoy should be read with our ears wide open to all the subtlety of their words and the complexity of their thought on the subject of peace and war. The same, I might add, is true of that other great writer who stands alongside Shakespeare and Tolstoy – the third of the three giants who have had such a powerful influence upon Western culture. I am referring to Homer, and to Homer's *Iliad*. There is a great deal in the *Iliad* about the virtues and benefits of peace as well as about the heroism and horrors of war. But that is the subject for another enquiry.*

*I have discussed Homer's approach in *The Iliad* to peace and war in *The Glorious Art of Peace* (OUP: 2012), pp. 40-47. Some passages in this talk are also based on the discussion of Shakespeare and Tolstoy in my book.

by Joy Shim
philosophicaljoy.wordpress.com

Britain's 1914-18 War Resisters

Cyril Pearce

The author compiled the Pearce Register of British Conscientious Objectors, which is available free online through the Imperial War Museum's Lives of the First World War website. Comrades in Conscience, *his acclaimed book about Huddersfield's opposition to the Great War, is published by Francis Boutle (£15, see Spokesman 128). A new book,* Communities of Resistance: Patterns of dissent in Britain during the First World War, *is forthcoming.*

For all historians of this last, most violent, century some concern with matters of war and peace has been unavoidable. However, a cursory glance at the shelves of any bookshop, whether on the High Street, the Imperial War Museum or the National Archive, and a flick through the pages of the *Pen and Sword* catalogue would leave the very strong impression that most writers' concerns, and their readers' too, have been about war rather than peace. It would appear that accounts of individual heroics, memorable war leaders, battles, regimental histories and the grim technology of killing in the twentieth century, are endlessly fascinating. Yet the antithesis of all this has not gone unexplored. Indeed, for a minority, frequently ignored or banished to the margin and, by some who ought to know better, dismissed as 'cranks', the men and women who made up Britain's 1914-18 anti-war movement have not wanted for historians. Since 1919, although in fits and starts, the historiography of war resisters and conscientious objectors has grown to a considerable body of work. Not all of it has been good, let alone innovative. There has been some re-working of old material here and there but that has been interspersed with genuinely new perspectives and some alternative insights. Nowhere has this been more true, if belated, than with new approaches drawn from the burgeoning field of women's history and feminist theory. As the changing emphases in historical scholarship have been reflected in work in this field, so have the broader political concerns with war and peace. The advent of computers, the internet, the digitisation of documents and the expiry of closure orders on First World War sources have revolutionised what can be done, and, with family and local historians in mind, who can do it. Historical research is no longer the special preserve of the Academy. As the First World War Centenary commemoration process rolls on, the emphasis on community involvement in Heritage Lottery funded projects looks set to create a different account of the war, especially on the Home Front. Informed by Family and Local History that 'different' account will have challengingly different points of departure and, inevitably, different conclusions.

Writing the history of Britain's 1914-1918 war resisters, arguably, began as early as 1919. The No-Conscription Fellowship (NCF), the organisation which had campaigned against the war, against conscription and in support of Conscientious Objectors (COs), published its own history of Britain's war resisters with *The No-Conscription Fellowship: A Souvenir of its work during the years 1914-1919*. A collection of essays by key figures in the NCF, it established, at least in outline, the narrative which informed much of the history written about the anti-war movement for the next fifty years. Valuable as an early attempt to voice the anti-war story, but as much a polemic as it was a history, it was a somewhat limited beginning. The real starting point was the work of John W. Graham (1859-1932). A former Mathematics Tutor, from 1897 to 1924 he was Principal of Dalton Hall, a Quaker hall of residence at Owen's College, later Manchester University. He was a prominent member of the Society of Friends, a writer on Quaker Theology and a very public peace advocate and supporter of Conscientious Objectors during the First World War. It was 'Principal' Graham who built on the outline established by the NCF's *Souvenir* history with his more substantial work: *Conscription and Conscience: A History 1916-1919*, (first published in 1922 by George Allen and Unwin, reprinted in facsimile by Augustus Kelly in 1969 and more recently by Forgotten Books, 2012). It was dedicated 'with affectionate reverence to the young men who in the dark days of the war kept the faith and stood by their country and mankind with a courage that did not fail'. Despite the similarity between this and the words on War Memorials across the country these words were not meant for the young men who served in the armed forces, but for those who refused to fight. What follows the dedication is an authoritative work of history but it is also a polemic aimed at the heart of the post-war debate on the legacy of the war and plans for a future peace. Clifford Allen's Preface to the book clearly has that in mind along with an appeal for a sympathetic understanding of the war resisters' position.

> The resister desires a new internationalism, by which States are conceived of less as embodiments of power and more as instruments of social administration. It should be the business of States to co-ordinate the free service of their citizens, and to compete in rivalry as to which can make the finest contribution to the stock of the world's happiness. In such a contest between nations, each would draw upon the special genius and wealth peculiar to its race and nationality.
>
> (Graham, p.23)

While Graham's work outlines and details the story of Britain's war resisters, its sub-text is nonetheless concerned elsewhere and with that bigger theme of war and peace, pacifism and conscience. Indeed, it is probably true to say that for at least fifty years after the publication of *Conscription and Conscience*, every attempt at writing about the First World War's war resisters has also been set against that bigger theme. That is not to say that acknowledging broader issues makes for bad history, far from it, but the finer detail is often obscured by the broad brush strokes of debate.

In the inter-war years and into the 1950s some of that finer detail was provided by the numerous biographies and autobiographies of war resisters and COs. Some, probably most of them, continued to combine history with polemic. One such key work, often dismissed and frequently under-valued, is E. Sylvia Pankhurst's *The Home front: A mirror to life in England during the First World War*. She described it as '… the story of my life and time during the war years 1914, 1915 1916 …' First published in 1932, and then again in 1987 by both Ebury and Century Hutchinson, it is, sadly, and surprisingly, no longer in print. If the first part of the book deals with her work with the poor in the East End of London, more that half of it deals with the anti-war movement and, unlike Graham, acknowledges the role of women war resisters.

Another essential book which complements Graham and combines history with polemic is *We did not fight: 1914-18 experiences of war resisters*. Published in 1935 by Cobden-Sanderson, it was edited by Julian Bell with a Foreword by Canon H. R. L. 'Dick' Shepherd. The year is not without significance. It was the year in which Shepherd founded the Peace Pledge Union, two years after the Oxford Union had voted that 'this House will not fight for King and Country', a time when the inherent militarism of German and Italian Fascism threatened Europe and a year before the Spanish Civil War reminded the world of the power of modern weaponry to kill and destroy soldiers and civilians alike. In this collection of essays along with those intentionally addressing the threats to peace are, as the sub-title suggests, personal accounts of the experiences of individual war resisters. Among them were Clifford Allen, David Garnett, Stephen Hobhouse, Bernard Langdon-Davies, James Maxton, James Millar, Bertrand Russell and John Rodker. Subsequently most of these found their biographers, and, in the case of Russell, several – of which, more later. Arthur Marwick, son of William, a Scottish CO who served time in prison and in a number of work centres, no doubt exorcised some of his own ghosts with his *Clifford Allen: Open Conspirator* (Oliver and Boyd, 1964). David Garnett and his then partner, also a CO, Duncan Grant, appear in some way in many of the accounts of the Bloomsbury Set, most usefully, for this present purpose, in Jonathan Atkin's *A War of Individuals: Bloomsbury Attitudes to the Great War* (Manchester University Press, 2002). Maxton, a controversial figure in the history of the political 'Left' in inter-war Britain has not lacked for biographers nor for key roles in books with wider concerns. He has a part in Willie Gallacher's, *Revolt on the Clyde : An autobiography* (Lawrence and Wishart, London, 1936) and is one of a galaxy of Glaswegian working-class heroes in Robert K. Middlemas' *The Clydesiders: A left wing struggle for Parliamentary power* (Hutchinson, London, 1965). He also appears in his own right in several biographies among them ones by John McNair, (Allen and Unwin, 1955), Gordon Brown (Edinburgh, Mainstream, 1986) and William Knox (Manchester University Press, 1987). But of the other contributors to that 1935 collection, John Rodker's writing offers some of the more intriguing insights into the CO experience. His autobiography was published anonymously in 1932 as *Memoirs of other fronts* (Putnam, London). In it, he describes attitudes and actions very different from the expected. He speaks of weekends with his lover in a hotel in Princetown while at Dartmoor prison Work Centre and vents a withering disdain for the religious COs who were disappointed that their prediction of the end of the world had not come true. He went on the run twice and after his final escape from Dartmoor to London's literary scene he survived unchallenged to the end of the war because the well-to-do literary society in which he moved was seldom troubled by the police.

At least three autobiographical accounts of CO experiences were published during the war as contributions to the debate about the war and the treatment of COs. T. Corder Catchpool, *On Two Fronts* (Headley Brothers, 1918) was one of them. It was a collection of his letters edited by his sister. Catchpool, a Quaker CO, served in the Friends' Ambulance Unit (FAU) from September 1914 to May 1916 but left to take a stand against conscription. He was refused absolute exemption from combatant service and found himself in the army. There, as an 'Absolutist' he refused to obey orders and refused all government schemes. Consequently having had four courts martial and four different sentences he spent two years in prison before his release in the spring of 1919. Unlike Rodker's account, his is a story of grace in adversity and high moral principle. The same is true of *'Handed Over': The Prison Experiences of Mr J Scott Duckers, Solicitor of Chancery Lane, under the Military Service Act, written by himself* (C. W. Daniel, London, 1916). Catchpool and Scott Duckers were cited by the NCF as 'Typical' Conscientious Objectors; Rodker was not. Another wartime CO memoir, published in 1918, was E. W. Mason's *Made free in Prison* (Allen and Unwin, London). Essentially an edited collection of Edward Williamson Mason's letter to his friend 'Harry', it is a close description of his CO experiences from his arrest in July 1916 to his second court martial at Catterick in July 1917 and his transfer to Northallerton prison. At the same time, they are as much an account of a spiritual journey as they are a political testimony.

These wartime memoirs apart, the first CO memoir to be published, in the inter-war years was probably George Baker's *The Soul of a Skunk: The autobiography of a Conscientious Objector* (Eric Partridge Ltd., the Scholartis Press, London, 1930). Dedicated to his son Paul, '… that he may know what his Daddy did in the war', he describes it as '… the story of a man who, then not much more than a boy, during the Great War did his bit for England as a pacifist in prison'. As with Richard Fox, it contains some of the more affecting CO writing of its time. A young bank clerk when war broke out,

> This book shows how one socialist, at least, was not born but made, It shows … how and why its subject became, not arbitrarily but inevitably, a pacifist, a Skunk, an Ishmael (except that his hand was not against all men's), who, before prison, wore the white feather; in prison the broad arrow, and, after prison (according to some) the badge of a matricide, the mark of Cain. It seeks to show how, as Rupert Brooke and Robert Graves would have sinned against the light that was in them had they gone to prison and not to France, so the Skunk would have sinned against the light that was in him, had he gone to France and not to prison.
>
> (Foreword p.ix)

Numerous other CO autobiographies were published, from the 1930s onwards. It is not possible here to list them all but a short selection can give an impression of their range and variety. Few of them are entirely devoted to their author's CO experiences, indeed, some are only too ready to skim over it. Most are records of busy lives actively engaged in political work.

One of the best written CO memoirs is R. M. Fox's *Smoky Crusade* (The Hogarth Press, London, 1938). Richard Morris Fox and his younger brother, Eric Lionel, lived in North London and were members of the North London Herald League. They were both Socialist COs and 'Absolutists'. Richard was an apprentice-trained engineer, a driller, who after the war went to Ruskin College, Oxford and became a writer and journalist. His account sets his experiences in the hectic context of social and industrial unrest, Ireland, revolutionary Russia and wartime Britain. His descriptions of Tribunal hearings, prison and hunger striking at Wandsworth rank among the best. If that is true for one of the generality of COs then it is equally true of the memoir of one of the anti-war movement's leaders, Archibald Fenner Brockway. His *Inside the Left: Thirty Years of Platform, Press Prison and Parliament* (Allen and Unwin, London, 1942, Spokesman, Nottingham, 2010) should probably be set alongside Graham's work as an authoritative version of the CO experience. While it is the personal account of a young man from a well-to-do family becoming a Socialist and a determined war resister and CO, it is also the story of a man who became the editor of the Independent Labour Party's (ILP) *Labour Leader*, founder of the NCF, and a post-war figure of some significance in the Labour Party and, eventually, in Parliament.

If some CO memoirs inadvertently verge on literature rather than autobiography there is other writing with more overt literary ambitions. This might be said of John Rodker's *Memoirs of other fronts* although the emphasis remains with the memoir. However, Edward Gaitens' *Dance of the Apprentices* (First published in 1948 by William McLellan & Co., re-printed in 2001 by Cannongate Books, Edinburgh), is intentionally fiction but based on personal experience. Gaitens, a CO from Glasgow, was imprisoned, rejected by the Home Office Scheme and sent back to Wormwood Scrubs until April 1919. The book, as with much of his other work, is more about Glasgow than it is a CO story. In that it is probably unique among CO memoirs.

Unique among CO memoirs is Max Plowman's *A Subaltern on the Somme in 1916* (E. P. Dutton & Co., New York, 1928). Unlike Siegfried Sassoon and Wilfred Owen whose revulsion at the war did not extend to their refusing to fight, Max Plowman was one of a handful of British army officers who resigned his commission after distinguished military service, became a CO and was court martialled. Another was the actor Miles Malleson. After brief service with the army in Malta he was invalided out in 1915 but, when he had recovered, he refused to serve as a conscript. Fortunately for him it was more convenient for the army to regard him as still unfit for service rather than to insist on his joining up. Consequently, he continued to work in the theatre. Two of his one-act plays, written in 1916, *D Company* and *Black 'Ell* (Hendersons, London), critical portrayals of army life, were banned by the Lord Chamberlain. Malleson left no memoir of his time as a war resister but his wife did. Constance Malleson also an actor with the stage name Colette O'Niel [sic], published her autobiography in 1931, *After Ten Years: A Personal Record* (Jonathan Cape, London). She may be better known as having been one of Bertrand Russell's lovers, but she was also as committed as her husband and, indeed, as Russell himself, to the anti-war cause. She did voluntary work for the No-Conscription Fellowship at its London headquarters and offers insights into its operation not seen anywhere else – as well as being an occasional visitor at Ottoline and Philip Morrell's gatherings of anti-war activists at Garsington Manor.

One of the more unlikely memoirs but, nonetheless a useful one, is that of Michael Isaac Lipman, usually referred to as 'Mick'. His *Memoirs of a Socialist Business Man* (Lipman Trust, 1980) offer insights into the political world of Leeds' pre-war and wartime radical community which other histories of Leeds ignore. His parents, originally from Russia, were secular non-practising Jews, atheists and anarchists. Visitors to their house were as likely to be from the Leeds Socialist Sunday School as they were to be the anarchists Guy Aldred, Rudolph Rocker or 'Red Emma' Emma Goldman. He offers a vigorous description of his own and his family's involvement in the anti-war movement. Three of his sisters married COs and although a schoolboy, he was arrested for distributing anti-war leaflets. He worked for the local branch of the NCF and the family home was used as a safe house for COs on the run.

Other memoirs, especially of the retired MP or Trade Union leader variety tend to be much less colourful. *Herbert Morrison: an autobiography*, attributed to Lord Morrison of Lambeth (Odhams Press, London, 1960) is a case in point. It is, as might be expected, concerned primarily with the grand sweep of a very significant political life. Perhaps for that reason the time he spent as a CO doing farm work near Letchworth occupies no more than two pages out of its 300. In comparison the autobiography of James Clunie (1888-1974), a Scots CO and Labour MP for Dunfermline from 1950 to 1959 has more to say about his stance as a CO. A former house painter, Socialist and Christian, he served one prison term before accepting the Home Office Scheme for work at Warwick, Dartmoor and Wakefield. The first volume of his two-part autobiography, *Labour is my faith: the autobiography of a house painter* (Dunfermline,

1954) has his reflections on his CO experience. For a simple description of life and work in Warwick and other work centres it has few equals. Arthur Horner (1894-1968), not an MP, but arguably an even more important figure in the Labour Movement as a lifetime member of the Communist Party and General Secretary of the National Union of Mineworkers (1946-1959), chose to give his memoir the title, *Incorrigible Rebel* (MacGibbon & Kee, London, 1960). It was a self-conscious reference to the words used at his sentencing after his second court martial in January 1919, '... discharged in consequence of incorrigible conduct ...' (p.9) A militant miner in the Welsh coalfield, originally exempt from military service as being in an essential occupation, he had crossed to Ireland to join Connolly's Irish Citizen's Army. In the summer of 1918 he was arrested as an absentee having returned from Dublin to see his wife and daughter.

One of the last CO memoirs, published in 1967, for his 90th birthday, was by Robert Stewart under the title, *Breaking the Fetters: The Memoirs of Bob Stewart* (Lawrence and Wishart, London). A Scot from Dundee and originally a full-time Temperance campaigner, like Arthur Horner, he was a convinced Communist and remained so to the very end. He resisted the war and conscription on class grounds and was court martialled four times. His unequivocal stance is clearly set out in a language of which modern politicians seem especially ignorant.

By the 1960s and 1970s, fifty or more years after the First World War, the original war resisters and Conscientious Objectors were beginning to slip away. Some leading figures lived on into their nineties. Bertrand Russell was still campaigning when he died in 1970 at the age of 97 and Fenner Brockway was only a few months short of his hundredth birthday when he died in 1988. Nevertheless, for most, by the 1970s memoir and autobiography had begun to give way to biography. But by this time mortality was not the only agent changing the way in which the history of Britain's 1914-18 war resisters was being written. Concerns about war and anxieties about how best to argue for peace persisted in the context of the Cold War and the nuclear arms race. At the same time questions about the future of radical politics in Britain were behind the creation of the *New Left Review* and the Society for the Study of Labour History. Scholarly concern for the origins and 'Forward march of Labour' inevitably touched on the matter of the First World War. Connected to all of that was the beginning of the expansion of Higher Education. By the 1960s significant numbers of young men and women from backgrounds where they were the first to go to university began to transform undergraduate and post-graduate History and to encourage it to reach out for new insights into Sociology and the broader Social Sciences. At the turn of the millennium, Labour and Social History had been broadened and enriched by Women's History and Gender Studies and this has been reflected in the work on the First World War's war resisters.

If the first fifty years of the historiography of the 1914-18 war resisters was dominated by a combination of John Graham's *Conscience and Politics* and the memoirs of its key figures, the last fifty years, leading up to the current centenary commemorations, have seen a great deal more research and writing across hitherto unexplored areas and with hitherto unexplored pre-occupations.

The passing of the men and women of the anti-war movement has prompted re-appraisal and tribute through biography. These might be divided into biographies of important or even 'celebrity' figures and those of the rest. Among those of the more modest or less well known are those of respected local figures. A case in point here is Wayne David's *Remaining True: A biography of Ness Edwards* (Caerphilly Local History Society, 2006). Edwards (1897-1968) was Labour MP for Caerphilly from 1939 until 1968. Although a miner who, like Arthur Horner, might have expected to be exempt from military service, he was called up but went on the run. He was not captured until the summer of 1918. After a prison sentence and some time at Dartmoor he went on the run again and didn't return home until 1919. The book is a homage by one Caerphilly Labour MP, Wayne David, to one of his predecessors.

That sense of 'homage' is never far from many CO biographies. In some it is a matter of a family history set in critical times. In *John Hoare: A Pacifist's progress – papers from the First World War* (Sessions Book Trust, York, 1998), Richard J. Hoare has edited his father letters and other writings to create a full and irresistible account of a Christian pacifist's CO story. It is true of *Philip W. Bagwell: Prison Cell to Council Chamber* (William Sessions, York, 1994), which was written by two of his children, Joan Lawley and her brother, the distinguished historian, Philip S. Bagwell. While Peggy Attlee wrote about her father in *With a quiet conscience: Thomas Simons Attlee 1880-1960* (Dove & Chough Press, London, 1995), and reminded us that Prime Minister and former Major Clement Attlee had a brother who took a rather different line. A similar labour of love combined with distinguished scholarship is to be found in John and Mary Postgate's celebration of their father in *A stomach for dissent: The life of Raymond Postgate, 1896-1971* (Keele University Press, 1994). This 'Writer, Radical Socialist and Founder of the Good Food Guide' defied his Tory father to take a stand as a CO. Alongside these, one of the more intriguing acts of family homage is Donald McNair's *A Pacifist at war: Military Memoirs of a Conscientious Objector in Palestine 1917-1918* (Anastasia Press, Much Hadham, 2008). It is based on his father Donald's letters to his wife. Donald was a CO, a devout Christian, who found himself in the Hampshire Regiment in Palestine, '… going over the top with a loaded rifle and fixed bayonet, yet determined not to fight …'. It is intriguing because it poses the question, if Donald McNair can be described as a CO although in the army and bearing arms, how many more were there like him?

The path from biography into broader historical themes is well trodden. The historiography of Britain's 1914-18 anti-war movement is no exception. Jo Vellacott remains the doyenne of this approach. Her *Bertrand Russell and the Pacifists in the First World War* (The Harvester Press, Brighton, 1980) now re-published with a 2015 Preface as *Conscientious Objection: Bertrand Russell and the Pacifists in the First World War* (Spokesman, Nottingham, 2015) sets Russell in context. It traces and describes his significant role in the anti-war movement at all its levels - his writings, his speeches to public meetings under the watchful eye of the secret services, his membership of the Executive Committee of the NCF and his six months imprisonment in 1918 for writings in the *Tribunal* which the authorities found dangerously subversive. Vellacott's work in this is a touchstone for the value of this approach. Nicholas Griffin's, *A Pacifist at War: Letters and Writings of Bertrand Russell 1914-1918* (Spokesman, Nottingham, 2014) takes a similar approach with a judicious and skilfully edited collection of Russell's writings set in a commentary on the history of the anti-war movement which is magisterially well-informed and written in a lucid and accessible way.

If Vellacott's work on Bertrand Russell and the anti-war movement has been seminal then so has her work on the women's movement and the war. Here her work on Catherine Marshall has contributed substantially to our revised understanding of the role of women in the anti-war movement. Marshall's work was acknowledged, if largely in passing by Graham, Fenner Brockway and others, but it has been Vellacott's work, directly from the original sources in Marshall's archive, which has enlarged and firmly substantiated her importance. Her *From Liberal to Labour with Women's Suffrage: The story of Catherine Marshall* (McGill-Queen's University Press, 1993) is essential to our understanding of the anti-war movement. Marshall is a substantial presence in *Bertrand Russell and the Pacifists* but it is in *From Liberal to Labour* that she is, and quite rightly, the central character. The logical and, at times, apparently organic progression in Vellacott's work from Russell to Marshall and then to wider reflections on the women's movement in the First World War is very apparent in her most recent work, *Pacifists, Patriots and the Vote: The erosion of democratic Suffragism in Britain During the First World War* (Palgrave McMillan, 2007). After reading this it is no longer possible to accept the earlier view that Emmeline and Christabel Pankhurst's super-patriotism was echoed in the rest of the women's movement.

Elsewhere there are other examples with different central characters. One of these is John Shepherd's *George Lansbury: At the heart of Old Labour* (Oxford UP, 2002). It is a scholarly and passionate account of Lansbury's path from local politics in London's East End to the Labour Leadership. A path informed by his Socialism, Christianity and pacifism. As editor of the pre-war *Daily Herald*, reduced to the weekly *Herald* during the war, he exercised an influence comparable to that once exercised by *The Clarion's* Robert Blatchford. The local branches of the Herald League were particularly influential in anti-war communities, especially North London. Although only touching briefly on his wartime contribution, Shepherd's work is essential to an understanding of how the spirit of opposition to war continued to inform British Labour politics in the inter-war years.

Perhaps more marginal but with a broader sense of humour is Ray Challinor's *John S. Clarke: Parliamentarian, Poet and Lion-tamer* (Pluto Press, London, 1977). It is one of the slimmer volumes (85 pages) but essential reading for those trying to understand the intersection between the 'Revolt on the Clyde', revolutionary socialism and the underground elements of the anti-war movement. If modern politicians can be accused of lacking a hinterland this could never be said of John S. Clarke. Beyond the pages of Challinor's slim volume, Clarke's writings published by Glasgow's Scottish Labour Press in 1919 as *Satires, Lyrics and Poems (Chiefly Humorous)* remain just as powerful, and just as funny, as they were a hundred years ago. More substantial in terms of the number of pages (290) and its content is John Taylor Caldwell's *Come Dungeons Dark: The Life and Times of Guy Aldred, Glasgow Anarchist* (Luath Press, Barr, Ayrshire, 1988). An important figure in the history of Anarchism in Britain and, despite his being born in London, in the history of Glasgow politics too, Aldred was a prominent, if controversial, Absolutist CO.

One of the more dramatic personal stories here is that of Derby's Alice Wheeldon. In 1917 she was a fifty-year-old mother with grown up children. A dealer in second-hand clothes, she was a Socialist, suffragette and anti-war campaigner. For reasons that were never made particularly clear, she and her daughters Winnie and Hettie and Winnie's husband Alf Mason were arrested on charges of planning to assassinate Lloyd George using poison. The case attracted national attention as, no doubt, was intended, and the accused found guilty. The fact that the prosecution's chief witness was a police spy who was not allowed to testify on the grounds of 'national security', was considered scandalous. Nevertheless, while Hettie was acquitted, Alice, Winnie and Alf were found guilty. Alice received the harsher sentence, ten years penal servitude while Alf and Winnie were given seven and five years respectively. Alice was an unco-operative prisoner and went on hunger strike. She was released in late December 1917, Winnie and Alf twelve months later.

The Wheeldon story is a paradigm of war resisters as victims of desperate, brutal and ultimately ruthless authorities and a supine and malleable legal process. It has been recognised as such in numerous general histories but it was Shelia Rowbotham in 1986 who saw its potential for illuminating a much bigger range of issues. Her *Friends of Alice Wheeldon* (Pluto Press, London) was originally a script for a play performed in 1980. But in its published form the script was accompanied by an innovative introductory essay dealing with 'Rebel Networks in the First World War'. Nicola Rippon's *The Plot to Kill Lloyd George: The story of Alice Wheeldon and the Pear Tree Conspiracy* (Wharncliffe Books, Barnsley, 2009) is more meticulous in its story telling but lacks Rowbotham's broader understanding.

The biographical route to an understanding of war resisters has, at times, produced work with ambiguous and not always sustainable pretentions. Will Ellsworth-Jones', *We will not fight ... the untold story of World War One's Conscientious Objectors* (Aurum, London, 2007) is not all its title claims. To begin with, the story of the World War COs is not 'untold' as much of what is written here would already suggest. Nor is Ellsworth-Jones' book the story of COs as a whole. It is, in fact, principally the story of one particular CO, 'Bert' Brocklesby, and of one specific set of circumstances in which he and 34 other COs found themselves. He was among those shipped out to France by the military authorities and sentenced to be shot for refusing to obey orders. The story is a good one, very well written and explained as never before but the story of the 35 'Frenchmen' is not the whole story of all those who said 'We will not fight'.

Rooted in the biographical approach but with more justifiable pretensions is Adam Hochschild's *To End All Wars: How the First World War divided Britain* (Macmillan, London, 2011). In a tour de force of exceptional writing he weaves together the personal wartime stories of a huge cast of people inevitably headed by Bertrand Russell but including '... feminists, trade unionists, aristocrats, future Members of Parliament ...' and a former editor, Fenner Brockway, '... who published a CO newspaper on toilet paper while he was in prison'. He follows a group of people, many connected by ties of family but who took different lines on the war including Sir John French and his sister Charlotte Despard and the Pankhursts. Beautifully written, it has a strong sense of the significance of the anti-war struggle and of the extent to which it divided British society at every level.

Those divisions remained very apparent at the mid-way point of the war's centenary and were reflected in print. The catalyst for much of that was David Boulton's *Objection Overruled: Conscription and Conscience in the First World War* (MacGibbon & Kee, London, 1967), now published with a revised Introduction by Dales Historical Monographs and the Friends' Historical Society (2014). It was originally published as a contribution to the 50th anniversary commemorations of the First World War 1964-1968. While drawing on what had gone before, especially on John Graham's work, Boulton brought new material to bear on the familiar story by adding the reminiscences of the many COs and their families who came forward offering their contributions in response to an appeal by Bertrand Russell and Fenner Brockway. The book is a vindication of that approach. Well written and passionate, even fifty years later it ranks alongside Graham's work as essential reading. A valuable companion volume to Boulton's work is Thomas C. Kennedy's *The Hound of Conscience: A History of the No-Conscription Fellowship, 1914-1919* (University of Arkansas Press, Fayetteville, 1981). While it lacks Boulton's broader concerns it is a meticulous exploration of the ways in which the NCF was held together during the war and the ways in which it managed to retain the engagement of the many and diverse elements of the anti-war community. Kennedy's essay on sources is particularly useful. Also useful as an adjunct to Boulton's work is Marvin Swartz's *The Union of Democratic Control in British Politics during the First World War* (Clarendon Press, Oxford, 1971). The UDC, along with the NCF was one of the organisations which the pro-war press loved to hate. It was essentially an elite national organisation with its own journal and an extensive network of local branches. Its aim was not to campaign against the war or even to support COs but, rather, to argue that decisions on war and peace should properly be taken by Parliament rather than government. That being the case the fact that many of its public meetings attracted violent mobs determined to break them up is a little strange.

Boulton's work, however, was not universally well-received when it first appeared in the late 1960s. Its very direct attack on the motives of both government and state institutions did not meet with general approval. Carrying the standard for those who sought to deflect or even deny Boulton's claims, especially those of the finer points of army brutality in the treatment of COs, was John Rae. His *Conscience and Politics: The British Government and the Conscientious Objectors to military service 1916-1919* (Oxford UP, 1970), well written and mostly well researched, still stands as the foremost apologia for the way COs were treated. Keith Robbins' *The Abolition of War: The 'Peace Movement' in Britain, 1914-1918* (University of Wales Press, Cardiff, 1976) is in much the same vein and others have followed suit. More recently James McDermott's work, *British Military Service Tribunals 1916-1918: 'A very much abused body of men'* (Manchester UP, 2011) is a review of the work of the Tribunal system. Based principally on the chance survival of the Northamptonshire Tribunal records and others it makes a timely and incontrovertible case by saying that the Tribunals were about more than just COs. There can be few quarrels with his findings there. However, in defending the Tribunals from the anti-war movement's criticisms, like Rae, he protests too much. They did indeed have a difficult job to do and, at times, without much guidance from central government, but that does not excuse the frequent abandonment of all sense of judicial impartiality exhibited in so many Tribunals when faced with the genuine claims of COs or, indeed, of others. Their shortcomings in this regard were not repeated in the Second World War when appeals for exemption from military service had to be made before a judge.

The question of how a liberal democracy should respond to internal criticism when faced with external threats remains relevant and the subject of sharp division. Brock Millman's work has addressed this dilemma head-on. *His Managing Domestic Dissent in First World War Britain* (Frank Cass, London, 2000) has a chillingly un-democratic ring to it. He describes the development in Britain of a panoply of powers available to government which, rather than being applied to the letter and consistently, never became more repressive than a working consensus of the population was prepared to tolerate, particularly where the anti-war movement was concerned. There were, of course, mistakes – the Wheeldon affair, the Birkenhead and Cleethorpes barracks brutality cases and the 35 COs sentenced to be shot in France – but, he argues, the relatively light touch applied by the authorities ensured that public opinion was not alienated.

The 'broader concerns' so evident in Boulton, Hochschild and Vellacott's work, characterise other approaches where the starting point is not so much the anti-war struggle as another theme. Dominant among these are the histories of political organisations, religious denominations and the women's movement.

Some political histories are more concerned than others with responses to and the effects of the First World War. The Liberal Party's crumbling as a national force under the impact of the war is described in most major texts on the political history of the time. Michael Howard's *War and the Liberal Conscience* (Oxford UP, 1981) subjects it to rather closer analysis. However, it is in the histories of the parties and factions of the 'Left' where the matter of the war looms much larger. This is particularly true of the ILP. It was the major partner in the Labour Party's coalition of partners before the adoption of its new constitution after 1918. Keith Laybourn's *The Century of Labour: A History of the Labour Party 1900-2000* (Sutton Publishing, Stroud, 2000) describes that structure and its response to the war. However, when war broke out the ILP's leaders, Philip Snowden, Ramsay McDonald, Keir Hardie and others, unlike the Parliamentary Labour Party, opposed Britain's involvement. ILP branches formed the core of most local anti-war organisations, especially the NCF and the National Council for Civil Liberties (NCCL), and ILP members were an important, if not the major, cohort in the ranks of COs. This is properly acknowledged in the appropriate histories – Robert E. Dowse, *Left in the Centre: The Independent Labour Party, 1893-1940* (Longmans, London, 1966) and David James et. al. (Eds.) *The Centennial History of the Independent Labour Party* (Ryburn Academic Publishing, Halifax, 1992). The difficulty with some of these accounts, however, is their mistaken tendency to project a particular reading of Bradford's ILP, where the anti-war stance appears to have been contended, onto the ILP elsewhere. Other work suggests that there might be different interpretations and that Bradford, while undeniably important, was not representative of the ILP as a whole. Such an alternative view is set out in Cyril Pearce's 'Shaping a Radical Community: Labour in West Yorkshire, 1906-1918' in Brendan Evans et.al. (Eds) *Sons and Daughters of Labour: A history and recollection of the Labour Party within the historic boundaries of the West Riding of Yorkshire* (University of Huddersfield Press, 2007).

The histories of Britain's Marxist 'Left' have different emphases. As its title suggests, Chushichi Tsuzuki's *H. M. Hyndman and British Socialism* (Oxford UP, 1961) takes the biographical route. Tsuzuki's pioneering work on this always controversial, early Socialist and patriot, inevitably is more concerned about his wartime stance than that of his opponents. In contrast Martin Crick's hugely authoritative *The History of the Social Democratic Federation* (Ryburn Publishing, Keele University Press, 1994), while acknowledging Hyndman's part, rightly stresses the importance of local membership in the British Socialist Party (BSP). It was the anti-war local members in 1916 who ousted Hyndman and the rest of the 'patriotic socialist' leadership and divided the party. Nevertheless, the role of those local members in leading their own war resister communities remains to be fully explored.

The emphasis in the work of Raymond Challinor and Walter Kendall is on the more overtly revolutionary Left. Kendall's *The Revolutionary Movement in Britain, 1900-1921: The Origins of British Communism* (Weidenfeld and Nicolson, London, 1969) is unequivocal in its intentions and makes a coherent story of the wartime and pre-war Left fragments which merged to form the Communist Party of Great Britain. Challinor's *The Origins of British Bolshevism* (Croom Helm, London, 1977) is also an original classic but owes more in its influences to the traditions of British Trotskyism and the divisions within the revolutionary Left than to anything else. Nevertheless, in their concerns to rescue the wartime stories of the war's more revolutionary opponents they do offer a contrasting picture to that offered by the NCF's 'Typical Conscientious Objectors'.

A sadly neglected approach, explored in detail only once to date, is that of the comparative study. We are lamentably ignorant of anti-war movements of Conscientious Objectors in the other European combatant countries. Francis L. Carsten (1911-1998) a German-born refugee from the Nazis, offered the first attempt at a comparative study with his *War against War: British and German Radical Movements in the First World War* (Batsford Academic, London, 1982). Something of that approach can be discerned in Peter Brock's *Against the Draft: Essays on Conscientious Objection from the Radical Reformation to the Second World War* (University of Toronto Press, 2006). This is a huge undertaking which explores the pacifist stance and the experience of Conscientious Objection at different times – from the 16th century to the 20th – and in very different countries and cultures. The mastery of detail in such a range of diverse and contrasting settings is excellent although, at times, it flags. The search for the broad general informing idea sometimes distracts from a proper understanding of the particular case. His essay on the British Non-Combatant Corps 1916-1918, for example, would have been stronger had it been rooted more closely in original sources.

Studies, such as Brock's, which look at pacifists and war resisters across time, places and cultures, are often driven by the need to identify a unified theme or a common element. That is frequently provided by reference to religious beliefs. To do that while, at the same time, characterising other motives as 'political' is to fly in the face of its inherent ambiguity. For example, how do we prioritise the anti-war stance of someone who claims to be both Christian and Socialist? Which comes first? All that we can say with any confidence is that significant numbers of war resisters claimed 'religious' motives even if, at the same time, claiming others.

Of those 'religious' war resisters there is little doubt that the Society of Friends, the Quakers, were both the most numerous and the most prominent. The Society's historic peace testimony remains an important part of its identity as does its members' continuing involvement in peace campaigning. The part played by the Friends' Ambulance Unit (FAU) in humanitarian work from 1914 onwards is well recorded. The Quaker commitment to truth and to record keeping has guaranteed that. Meaburn Tatham and James E. Miles produced its first history as early as 1919 in *The Friends' Ambulance Unit, 1914-1919: A Record* (Swarthmore Press, London). Geoffrey Winthrop Young, one of its founders, added an autobiographical note in his *The Grace of Forgetting* (Country Life, London, 1953). Nor has the work of that other Quaker humanitarian effort, the Friends' War Victims Relief Committee, gone unrecorded. Its General Secretary from 1914 to 1923, A. Ruth Fry, was its first historian, publishing in 1926 *A Quaker Adventure: The story of nine years' relief and reconstruction* (Nisbet & Co., London). Added to that, a good number of Quaker COs and FAU personnel chose to set down their own accounts of their experiences. While the evidence for the Quaker role in the anti-war movement is incontrovertible, some reservations about its interpretation have begun to appear. Thomas C. Kennedy's *British Quakerism, 1860-1920: The transformation of a Religious Community* (Oxford UP, 2001) firmly established what we now recognise as the Quaker role, not just in opposition to war, but at the forefront of many of the twentieth century's progressive movements. However, while doing that, he raised the question of just how resilient the peace testimony might have been when challenged by the demands of patriotism in 1914. The Society's own records show that almost a third of eligible Quaker men actually joined up and served with the rest. Kennedy's work on the 'War Quakers', as they were known, has helped dispel the image of an unchallenged Quaker witness for peace. Indeed, in his 2014 Presidential Address to the Friends' Historical Society, David Rubinstein, used this to counsel against complacency as the Society thought how it might best commemorate the centenary of the First World

War. Quakers may have been prominent war resisters, he argued, but a significant minority of them were not and their wartime experience ought not to be ignored.

Few other religious communities were defined as clearly by the war. Indeed most established denominations, with the exception of the Church of England, refused to draw that theological line. Individual churchmen, irrespective of their denomination, could be found on both sides of the argument. Even in the Church of England, officially the 'National' church and, therefore, nominally at least, committed to the war, there were deep divisions. A broad survey of the Church of England in wartime within which war resisters play hardly any part is to be found in Alan Wilkinson's *The Church of England and the First World War* (SPCK, London, 1978 and SCM Press, London 1996). Clive Barrett's more recent work, *Subversive Peacemakers: War resistance 1914-1918, an Anglican perspective* (Lutterworth Press, Cambridge, 2014) tells another story. Based on original research and using an impressive range of sources, he skilfully draws on poetry, memoirs, letters and personal testimony to describe an Anglican contribution to the pre-war peace movement previously only guessed at. It is a masterful and passionately told story of war resistance previously disregarded or undervalued in the unlikely setting of the Church of England.

For the individual Christians in denominations which refused to take a clear line on the war there was the Fellowship of Reconciliation (FOR). It was founded in late 1914 as a committed Christian and determinedly non-political anti-war organisation which since then has expanded to become the International Fellowship of Reconciliation (IFOR) while retaining its national branches. Its members included the whole spectrum of Christian denominations. Probably the most comprehensive account of its contribution is Jill Wallis' *Valiant for Peace: A history of the Fellowship of reconciliation, 1914-1989* (FOR, London, 1991). In 2014 it published another, more concise version of its history as *Fellowship of Reconciliation, Non-violence in action: 100 Years of Peacemaking* (FOR, London).

Never one to miss the opportunity to take a pot shot at those who regarded the anti-war movement as dominated by Quakers and Socialists, John Rae gleefully drew attention to the fact that more than 2,000 COs, maybe 10% or more of the total, can be identified as coming from minority religious sects. Among them were Plymouth Brethren, Seventh Day Adventists, Peculiar People, Pentecostalists, Spiritualists, Christian Israelites and a great many more. Most numerous were the

Christadelphians. Perhaps 1,700 or more were exempt from military service and allowed to do work of national importance in various sections of the economy, most controversially in munitions. The exemption was the result of a deal struck between the leaders of the Christadelphian community, in particular, Frank Jannaway, and the War Office. In return for exemption from military service Christadelphians of military service age were to be policed by their leaders and delivered to war essential work. The theological justification for this is to be found in the sect's firm belief that it is not of this world but of God's and that at the end of days its members would be among the elect. Jannaway's account of the deal with government is set out in his *Without the camp: Being the story of why and how the Christadelphians were exempted from military service* (Privately printed for Christadelphian subscribers, London,1917).

Less is known of the other minority faiths with significant numbers among the ranks of COs. Mark Sorrell has written an excellent guide to *The Peculiar People* (Paternoster Press, Exeter, 1979) but, websites apart, the other sects have yet to find their historians. The histories which do exist and are posted on websites tend to be as much devotional and proselytising as they are history. The exception is probably Gary Perkins' account of the stance taken by the members of the International Bible Students, pre-cursors of the Jehovah's Witnesses and posted as www.forthesakeofthekingdom. Also online is a brief account of the 7th Day Adventist COs at www.adventist.org.uk/wwi/ww1.

The use of language and concepts more often used in discussions of religious belief has been a common and much-published part of the historiography of war resisters. David A. Martin's *Pacifism: A Historical and Sociological Study* (Routledge & Kegan Paul, London, 1965) set the trend by approaching the study of war resisters within the intellectual framework set by the sociology of religion. In 1980 Martin Ceadel continued the theme with his *Pacifism in Britain 1914-45: The defining of a faith* (Oxford University at the Clarendon Press, 1980). Indeed, much of his very extensive and intellectually stimulating output since then has extended and explored further his engagement with pacifism in its many forms as well as with its organisation and practices: *Thinking about Peace and War* (Oxford UP, 1989; *Semi-detached idealists: The British Peace Movement and International Relations, 1845-1945* (Oxford UP, 2001) and his *Living the Great Illusion: Sir Norman Angell, 1872-1967* (Oxford UP, 2009).

Other studies of anti-war movements in the 20th century have set aspects of Britain's 1914-18 war resisters in a much broader worldwide process.

Caroline Moorhead's *Troublesome People: Enemies of war, 1916-1986* (Hamish Hamilton, London, 1987) begins with 'defining the faith' of 1916's COs, travels by way of the 1930s and the cold war to a reflection on the Greenham Common protest and the continuing importance of the peace movement as an assertion of individual freedom against the overwhelming power of the state. The collection of essays in *Campaigns for Peace: British Peace Movements in the twentieth century* (Manchester UP, 1987) edited by Richard Taylor and Nigel Young is in much the same vein. On the other hand, the diversity of its component essays, most of them by peace scholars, academics and activists, makes for a much richer and illuminating reading. James Hinton's *Protests and Visions: Peace Politics in 20th Century Britain* (Hutchinson Radius, London, 1989) covers similar ground but primarily as a way of describing the continuity of the peace movement and the roots of the Campaign for Nuclear Disarmament (CND).

The worldwide importance of pacifism as a state of mind and a political statement has probably been best explored in the work of Peter Brock and Nigel Young. Their *Pacifism in the Twentieth Century* (University of Toronto Press, 1999) ranges from First World War COs via Gandhian non-violence to studies of 'New' Conscientious Objectors in a number of different countries from the 1960s onwards, and to the more recent development of a more clearly articulated religious pacifism. The ambition of that worldwide reach is to be commended as, indeed, is that of its successor, the *Oxford International Encyclopaedia of Peace* (Oxford UP, 2010). For its editor, Nigel Young, it is a monumental piece of work and a fitting tribute to a career spent in 'Peace Studies'.

Notwithstanding all that has been described above, the major change in our understanding of Britain's 1914-18 war resisters, as in so much else, has come from the new perspectives provided by Women's History and Gender Studies. The publication of Sheila Rowbotham's *Hidden from History* (Pluto Press, London) in 1973 and the broad advance of the women's movement in the intervening years have resulted in the undeniable insistence on the need to redress the imbalance in historical scholarship by addressing women's role. Jo Vellacott's work on Catherine Marshall and Sheila Rowbotham's *Friends of Alice Wheeldon* have already been mentioned. They have been major parts of this process. Along with them, and in some cases preceding them have been others. One of the earliest, Sylvia Pankhurst excepted, was Gertrude and Bussey and Margaret Tims' *Pioneers for Peace: Women's International League for Peace and Freedom, 1915-1965* (WILPF, British Section, London, 1965 and 1980). It was published originally to mark the 50th anniversary of the creation of WILPF but stands rather more significantly than that, beginning with the International women's conference at the Hague in 1915, as the first account of the work of a women's organisation, eventually international, to campaign for peace and against war. If this has the feel of a slightly measured and dispassionate institutional history, then Anne Wiltshire's *Most Dangerous Women: Feminist peace campaigners of the Great War* (Pandora, London, 1985) is the opposite. Dedicated 'To Greenham women everywhere' it examines the 1915 Hague conference rather more closely and does not stint to describe the horrified abuse levelled at these 'Dangerous Women' by their male contemporaries. Similar accounts of men's abuse of the women who made a stand for their rights and for peace is not unknown in Jill Liddington's work. Since the publication in 1978, of her first book, *One Hand Tied Behind Us: The Rise of the Women's Suffrage Movement* (Virago) she has doggedly and with huge success pushed back the boundaries of our understanding of the nature and impact of women engaged in the social and political life of Britain in the 20th century. Her contributions to understanding the women's role as 1914-18 war resisters have come in two forms. The first was her biography of one of Lancashire's 'political' women, suffragist and peace activists in *The Life and times of a Respectable radical: Selina Cooper, 1864-1946* (Virago, London, 1964). Although concerned mostly with the whole sweep of Selina Cooper's life, its brief account of her involvement with the Women's Peace Movement and of a near-disastrous anti-war meeting in Nelson, is telling. The second, wholly centred on women and the peace movement is her *The Long Road to Greenham: Feminism and anti-militarism in Britain since 1820* (Virago, London, 1989). The book's concern was to connect the women's Greenham protest for peace and against cruise missiles, with a much older peace movement. Hitherto, with some exceptions, the history of the British peace movement, it argues, had not credited women with a role. The *Long Road to Greenham* began the process towards a proper identification of women's contribution. Since then, it might be said, accounts of the contributions made by engaged and politically active women have become commonplace. They have even added something of that comparative dimension missing elsewhere. Alison Fell and Ingrid Sharp's *The Women's Movement in Wartime: International Perspectives, 1914-1919* (Palgrave McMillan, Basingstoke, 2007) is an excellent example of this hitherto undeveloped perspective. Sybil Oldfield's collection of essays, *'Thinking Against the Current': Literature and Political Resistance* (Sussex Academic Press, Brighton, 2015) is another stimulating case in point. In its twenty-one essays women or women's concerns are central whether in the late 17th or early 21st century. Inevitably it deals with women and war from the First World War to the present.

Women's History has not simply been about adding the women's story where it had previously been left out. It has been the major driver of work and thinking across the whole range of academic activity that has come to be called Gender Studies. The understanding of the ways in which society creates expectations of behaviour specific to gender has been of major significance to scholarship as much as it has been to everyday life and popular culture. Jessica Meyer's *Men of War: masculinity and the First World War* (Palgrave McMillan, Basingstoke, 2009) has been important in applying that approach to the history of the First World War. Where the study of First World War COs is concerned one of the more original contributions has come from this source. With her *Telling Tales about Men: Conceptions of Conscientious Objectors to Military Service during the First World War* (Manchester UP, 2009), Lois Bibbings has taken the language and images used to describe COs whether in the press, in government propaganda or on public platforms and has examined the ways in which it was used to create a popular image. That the image was of 'unmen', cowards, shirkers even criminal deviants, made COs to be outsiders, 'other', much in the way that societies characterise other minorities the better to deny them their rights and liberty. It is a powerful argument and one which has resonance beyond the First World War.

The concerns of Women's History and Gender Studies may well be said to be drivers of a great deal of modern historical scholarship. However, there is still far too little activity where these two themes intersect with local and regional studies of Britain during the First World War. One notable exception to that is Alison Ronan's *'A Small Vital Flame': Anti-war women in North West England, 1914-1918* (Scholar Press, 2014). Based on a wide reading in the relevant literature, its strength is its use of a rich deposit of local source material for Manchester and its region. That material, seldom so thoroughly worked, demonstrates the strength of the women's movement beyond the narrow confines of London and the South East and away from the control of the women's movement's pro-war patriots. It also demonstrates the importance of the need for local counterbalances to the lazy historic assumptions of the existence of a uniform 'national mood'.

Possibly the first work to contradict the assertions that from 1914 to 1918 there had been a 'national' consensus in favour of war was Ken

Weller's *'Don't be a soldier!' The Radical anti-war movement in North London, 1914-1918* (Journeyman, London, 1985). It is an account of the anti-war movement in the North London boroughs of Islington, Hackney, Stoke Newington and parts of Middlesex. Its ideological centre was the North London Herald League and an eclectic combination of Socialists and trade unionists. Like David Boulton's *Objection Overruled* it is based on a mix of local sources, family papers and oral testimony. That mix produces a very different view from the one based on official and institutional sources. If it is to be criticised it is that it has little to say about the women's contribution.

Weller's work has been influential in encouraging others to look more closely at their local war resisters. Unfortunately this has not been reflected in the volume of other similar work. To date there is only one comparable local study, Cyril Pearce's *Comrades in Conscience: The story of an English community's opposition to the Great War* (Francis Boutle, London, 2001 and 2014). In this case the community is Huddersfield in West Yorkshire and, as with Weller's work, the study is based on a range of local sources informed by family papers and oral testimony. It describes a local anti-war community which united political elements from the Left with the women's movement and well-to-do Quakers to create a community which, although a minority, was influential in local attitudes to the war. It also describes an anti-war culture which persisted into the inter-war years. That this and Weller's work have challenged old assumptions about popular attitudes to the war has been recognised in more recent general histories such as Adrian Gregory's much-praised *The Last Great War: British Society and the First World War* (Cambridge UP, 2008) and even, perhaps surprisingly, given its title, in Catriona Pennell's *A United Kingdom: Popular Responses to the Outbreak of the First World War in Britain and Ireland* (Oxford UP, 2012).

After all this, what next? The First World War's centenary commemorative period, 2014 to 2018, has begun to create its own dynamic. Outside the 'official' acts of commemoration, organisations of all kinds are discovering ways of creating their own centenary histories. Inevitably these are dominated by the stories of soldiers and the communities from which they came. The battlefield honours of local regiments, local heroes and medals awarded are much to the fore. There is also an emphasis on the home front, the role of women and the contribution of local industry and agriculture. But within this activity there are groups and individuals, some representing organisations such as Quakers, branches of CND or even the Peace Pledge Union, who are researching local war resisters.

That commemoration activity has already begun to produce its own work, and it continues. Watford's Quakers have produced their own DVD, *Watford's Quiet Heroes: Resisting the Great War*, based on the experiences of local COs. A story simply but tellingly told by Simon Colbeck with contributions from Jo Vellacott and David Boulton. The Oswestry Coalition for Peace has published a collection of extracts from CO writings with the title, *When Men Refuse to Fight: writings on peace and conscientious objection 1914-1919* (Oswestry Coalition for Peace, 2014). More substantially, and with the support of the Heritage Lottery Fund, Leicester Campaign for Nuclear Disarmament (CND) have produced an impressively researched and splendidly illustrated account of Leicester and Leicestershire COs. Written by the Leicester Memories in Conflict Collective, their *Uncovering Resistance: Leicester and Leicestershire in World War One* (Leicester CND, 2015) might usefully act as a model for other similar projects. If these are products of the combined efforts of groups of enthusiasts, the work of the independent researcher/writer is not unrepresented. Two books, by two very different writers and about two very different parts of Britain, have added their own contributions to this growing body of work. Philip Adams has followed the history of his home town, *A Most Industrious Town: Briton Ferry and its people 1814-2014* (Philip Adams, Ludlow, 2014) with an equally authoritative account of its anti-war movement in his *Not in Our Name: War and dissent in a Welsh Town* (Philip Adams, Ludlow, 2015).

Industrial South Wales is a world away from the small Leicestershire town of Lutterworth, the focus of Andy Ward's explicitly titled book *Conchies: The Uncomfortable story of the Payne Brothers: Conscientious Objectors in the First World War* (Matador, Kibworth Beauchamp, Leicestershire, 2015). It is a work of very clear obsession which, sadly, Andy did not live to see in print. In more than 450 pages with almost as many detailed footnotes as text, it explores and, it has to be said, struggles with, the question of conscientious objection, when set alongside the experience of military service and suffering. The focus of the work is the story of the two Payne brothers, religious COs from a moderately prosperous family of basket makers. Lutterworth's only COs, they and their family became the targets of sustained victimisation from their first appearance before the local Tribunal in 1916, culminating on the evening of the 28th May 1918 in an attack on their home and workshop by a mob which grew to almost a thousand. The task of preserving order was beyond the two policemen who found themselves at the scene. They helped the family escape to safety in a neighbour's house but could not prevent the mob from smashing all the windows in the Paynes' house and shop or to prevent them from making a bonfire of the shop's contents and from setting fire to its warehouse and workshop. It is a story told in graphic details with the use of an enviable array of sources – Payne family papers amongst them – which struggles at length to explain why the people of Lutterworth might have descended to this frightening violence but stops well-short of passing judgement. Other writers may not have been so understanding.

Perhaps, when the commemoration period has run its course, the catalogue of work will be even more extensive. Some of it – exhibitions, lectures, conferences and discussions - will be more ephemeral. Nevertheless, the signs are promising. By the spring of 2015 the Heritage Lottery Fund had already supported more than fifteen First World War commemorative projects which were either wholly or in part concerned with COs. Others are coming forward. Independent researchers and local groups are pressing ahead without outside funding and a handful of Ph.D. students are already at work. The hope is that when all of this activity is completed we will have two important things: first a series of local studies which are made by local people and owned by them and second, perhaps a greater ambition, a history of the war and its war resisters, for the first time, written from below and with a concern for the experiences of people where they lived. If these can be achieved then the result may be a 'National Story' of Britain's war resisters informed by the full rich diversity of local histories which, again for the first time, properly balances the traditional received wisdom.

An earlier version first appeared in the Institute of Historical Research's online journal Reviews in History
(http://www.history.ac.uk/reviews/review/1779).

The Pearce Register can be accessed via
http://blog.livesofthefirstworldwar.org/conscientious-objectors-in-the-first-world-war/

See 'Cranks and Kites' p.99 ➤

THE BANNING OF BERTIE
BRITAIN'S GREATEST LIVING PHILOSOPHER
BERTRAND RUSSELL, WAS BANNED UNDER THE
DEFENCE OF THE REALM ACT FROM A THIRD
OF THE COUNTRY FOR AN ANTI-WAR
SPEECH HE MADE IN CARDIFF
ON 6TH JULY 1916

Reviews

Dig for Plenty

Lesley Acton, *Growing Space: a History of the Allotment Movement,* 270 pages, Five Leaves Publications, 2015, paperback ISBN 9781910170137, £14.99

Growing Space deals overwhelmingly with the 20th century history of the allotment movement. An earlier period, 1793 to 1873, is covered in a book by Jeremy Burchardt, which the author mentions in the acknowledgements as the inspiration behind her writing of the present highly readable and informative work. The allotment movement has ebbed and flowed, reflecting the changes in society and the material condition of the mass of the population. The Industrial and Agricultural Revolutions' impact on population distribution was, of course, profound, with Britain moving from a largely rural to a predominantly urban society, and this change ushered in the allotment both in its rural and urban forms.

Land enclosure, which had commenced in Tudor times, had nearly finished in the last years of Queen Victoria's reign. By the end of the 19th century, the allotment, whether as compensation for the rural poor's loss of common land or as a utilitarian dietary supplement and recreational activity for the city dweller, had become an important feature of the nation's life. Certainly, the allotment's popularity is a response to the clamour of urban existence, even now. If one has not got the money to 'flee to the country' then, undoubtedly, the allotment provides an inexpensive alternative.

The first chapter of *Growing Space* gives a brief overview of the period, noting, before launching into a detailed, mainly chronological series of chapters, that the number of allotments, their ups and downs, mirror changes in the attitudes and the requirements of the nation. The author charts these oscillations, placing them in historical context in an interesting and informative way. The tussles with the state, both in its local and centralised manifestations, form a key element of *Growing Space*, highlighting some of the connections and ramifications for society at large.

Allotment numbers rose fairly dramatically during wartime, and the 20th century, unfortunately, saw two world wars. As a large proportion of Britain's food supply was and is from imports, and as the war at sea was costly in lives and ships, 'Digging for Victory' was no idle slogan. At other times, the class war also impacted on the allotment movement, for example in 1928, with the Quakers playing a crucial role in setting up the Coalfields Distress Committee, which was to make available food for unemployed miners' families through 'providing and restoring' allotment sites.

Throughout the 20th century, the allotment movement had its friends and enemies. When it came to government, both local and central, whether it was as friend or foe often depended on what ministerial hat was being worn. In turn, the authorities' relationships with the allotment movement were often dependent on commercial pressures. Local authorities may have coveted land for 'development', which often meant housing, while other more sympathetic local authorities were keen to protect and extend allotments, not least for the health of the community. Throughout the period between the two world wars, unemployment remained stubbornly high, as did the consequent demand for allotments.

With the outbreak of the Second World War, the importance of allotments was immediately recognised by national government and, at its conclusion, the demand for allotments was unabated with the slogan 'Dig for Victory' changed to 'Dig for Plenty'. In 1945, the new Labour Government had to replace the bombed housing stock as well as beginning the mammoth task of slum clearance. As a result, the need for house building land came into direct conflict with the desire for allotments. Not only that – there was also bomb damage to allotments, particularly in the London area. TNT residue and bomb craters were of little use to gardeners! Shortages and rationing continued for some years after the conclusion of hostilities, and confirmed the importance of the allotment as a source of fresh produce. During the war, many parks were given over to allotments in grassy areas, and now people were keen to restore the play areas to grass.

Disputes over allotments between the authorities and holders have always been numerous. To give just one local example: a Nottingham allotment site was threatened with closure as the land was to be allocated by the council to a local cycle manufacturer, as a distribution hub, given the site's proximity to the M1. After several visits to the courts, a compromise was agreed, but in the end the cycle company chose another site and the old allotment site was left abandoned for nearly 10 years. The last century saw some seven Allotments Acts passed by Parliament. The last one, enacted in 1950, recorded just over a million plots, and it is this Act which is largely the one in force today.

The 1960s was a period of decline for the allotment movement. As the property sharks circled the prime sites, the loss of members financially weakened the National Allotment and Garden Society and, thus, its ability to defend sites from closure. From 1950 to 1965, the number of allotment plots fell by roughly half, but numbers picked up in the 1970s and the early 1980s. The environmental movement in particular provided a fillip, and new members joined who were concerned about modern methods of farming. The BBC's *Gardeners' World* and other recent television programmes have actively promoted allotments. These ideas of working together collectively, of relating to the local community (often by association with local schools), of green spaces in grey urban environments, food which is fresh and has low transport costs, and the provision of interesting work carried out at one's own pace, underpin the allotment movement.

The last chapter on the culture of allotments is provokingly thoughtful, discussing the politics of the movement together with more mundane matters such as the 'shed'. Allotments have a long and proud history and are a 'dynamic part of contemporary life'. *Growing Space* records the vicissitudes of the allotment movement with considerable insight and detail, and stands as a useful contribution to the social history of the 20th and early 21st century. The publishers are to be thanked for bringing this book into the public domain and for the intelligent use of colour photographs, which enliven the text. *Growing Space* shows the allotment movement is very much alive and that there is much we can all learn from it, and much we might have to learn with the looming threat of climate change.

John Daniels
Bulwell allotment holder

Vital Byron

Richard Lansdown (editor), *Byron's Letters and Journals: A New Selection*, Oxford University Press, 2015, 560 pages, hardback ISBN 9780198722557, £30

Admirers of Lord George Gordon Noel Byron generally fall into two camps: those who adore his poetic output, and those fascinated by his uncompromising, chaotically romantic life. Those who consider themselves in the former camp may find their man within the astonishing lines of *Childe Harold's Pilgrimage* or the cantos of *Don Juan*. Those in the latter could do worse than delve into this selection of letters and journals by the original holder – 150 years before The Beatles – of the suffix '*-mania*', to flesh out their hero.

The editor, Richard Lansdown, rather gamely sets himself as a hostage to fortune with introductory gusto, quoting his 19th Century Byron archivist predecessor, Rowland Prothero:

> 'Byron's letters appeal on three special grounds to all lovers of English Literature: they offer the most suggestive commentary on his poetry; they give the truest portrait of the man; they possess, at their best, in their ease, freshness and racy vigour, a very high literary value'.

Byron's letters are not mere scribblings, juvenilia, or words best left for the eyes of their recipients. They are an essential element of not just the Byron canon, but also of something wider: equal to and surpassing

> 'Keats' letters, Coleridge's notebooks, and De Quincy's *Confessions of an English Opium Eater* … Pepys' diary and Boswell's journal'.

Does Lansdown's selection justify his bold claims?

A smattering of letters from Byron's youth opens the anthology, as he arrives at Newstead Abbey, Nottinghamshire, in the English Midlands, seemingly lonely and nervous at his new role as heir to the Byrons' ancestral home. Freudians will have a field day with his pleas for attention sent to his mother; while more salacious eyes will scan keenly the notes to his half-sister; each with its own desperate sense of longing. Readers of *The Spokesman* will, perhaps, seek out the Byron who fascinated Russell: the humanist, the pacifist, the rebel. You will not be disappointed.

Why has Byron endured as a contemporary hero, while contemporaries such as Shelley are seen as fixed in their time? 'Byronesque' is a catch-all for the poetic radical; the revolutionary who buckled his swash with a breath-taking, sexually charged élan? Outside certain cloisters of impeccably mannered academics, where does 'Shelleyesque' strike chords? We do him a great disservice when we call him the 'rock star of his day'; those mass-adored strutting peacocks, from Jagger onwards, owe a debt to Byron, rather than vice versa. When it came to moistening gussets and stiffening boned breeches, even the most dedicated bohemian musician falls short of this platonic idealisation.

Lansdown's introduction to the two year period following Byron's return to England from his Grand Tour, in the Summer of 1811, is particularly enlightening, showing that, while Byron seldom had a dull month, this particular period was defining: his political career; his first publishing breakthrough; and, of course, his scandalous and public affair with Lady Caroline Lamb, thrust him into the limelight.

Many friends, and his mother, died in a short period of time. Byron's ensuing melancholy seems to ferment into something potent, an intoxicant that never let go. '*A curse hangs over me and mine*' Byron writes to a friend in August 1811, *'I am almost desolate – left almost alone in the world'*. Sodden with grief, he takes up politics, claiming his seat in the House of Lords. Of course, being Byron, this is done kicking against the comfortable status quo. His maiden speech on the 'Frame Work' bill – not included here, but easily found elsewhere – is one of the finest pieces of political oratory ever heard in those chambers; a passionate defence of the Luddites, who sought to defend their livelihoods as hosiery makers, and an attack on those who advocated execution and violence to quell them. '*I have seen the state of the miserable men, and it is a disgrace to a civilized country'*, Byron explains to his political mentor, Henry Vassall-Fox, on the eve of the speech. Amusingly, Byron engages in a little behind-the-scenes chicanery to ensure his message is heard elsewhere, sending his anonymous '*Ode to the Framers of the Frame Bill'* to *The Morning Chronicle*. '*Of course, do not put my name to the thing*', he tells the editor.

Byron's political career re-emerged years later, when he was further radicalised into direct action. But his time in the Lords was short-lived, for the surprisingly rapid success of *Childe Harolde* came soon after. Byron had arrived; returning from his travels, yet covered with grief, somehow liberated the good Lord's mind, giving impetus to his stab at immortality. The poet was born.

The 'Mad, Bad and Dangerous to Know' tag might have seen Byron hounded out of the country, but it has done more to keep his legacy vital than he could ever have dreamt.

When Nottingham decided to bid for recognition as a UNESCO City of Literature, in 2014, Byron became central to celebrating its 'Rebel Town' history: alongside the original 'Angry Young Man', Alan Sillitoe, and that prickly challenger of social hypocrisy, D H Lawrence. Harnessing that spirit, which has commonality from Newstead to Nepal, is a much different approach to that of the dozen cities recognised so far. Byron forms part of Nottingham's radical continuum that flashes through history: the English Civil War; the Luddites; burning down Nottingham Castle in 1831 when the resident aristocrat, the Duke of Newcastle, voted against widening the franchise.

Greece and the financial crisis is, perhaps, the latest manifestation of Byron's continuing relevance. *'Greece; it is the only place I was ever contented in*', he wrote in June 1823, before embarking for the Ottoman-occupied country, after a long stay in Italy began to engender a sense of ennui. Arriving at Missolonghi, Byron was greeted as the saviour, but later succumbed to fever. His physician bled him repeatedly, as was the practice of the time. Sepsis probably set in and, weakened by cuts, he died. A comparison with the financial crisis is almost scarily analogous: Greece, a weakened but recovering body, subjected to deeper cuts, hurtling closer to the grave. One of the most romantic of all the statues of Byron stands close to the Greek Parliament in Athens: Byron, foot un-clubbed and hair perfectly tousled, is crowned by Greece, a chiselled, noble woman. From his outcry against the theft of the Elgin Marbles (Byron was very much opposed to Elgin's desecration of the Parthenon: see *The Curse of Minerva*) to his hatred of tyranny, Byron has become an enduring archetype of the poetic hero: living fast, dying young, leaving a good-looking corpse.

The annotations are generous, and Lansdown's introductions to each chapter are comprehensive and contextualising, often with an unsparing aside: Lady Caroline Lamb and Lady Byron, among others, are described unequivocally as *'dysfunctional and humourless admirers ... self-interested fabricators'*. The rather Spartan index is, therefore, a mild disappointment, though a good way to find a chewy morsel. '*Byron: diet*' brings up some fascinating ruminations on his antipathy to wine *'... it makes me savage and suspicious'*, before castigating himself for being so precious about his habits – '*Excuse this old woman's letter*'. '*Byron: animals*', with a staggering 17 entries, ranging from his early love of horses to his Newfoundland dog, Boatswain, the truest love of his life, to his more eccentric purchases – an ugly, tailless guard dog he named Mutz; numerous 'charming' monkeys; tortoises, and just about anything else furred, feathered or scaled; to an anecdote he relates of an elephant getting free in Venice – '*mad for want of a She, it being the rutting month*', eventually being bought down by cannon shot: all observed from the safety of a gondola. The inclusion of such nuggets elevates this book from a scholarly tome on Byron; it drips with contemporary and geographic colour.

For those seeking a decent reference book about Byron, then this is our generation's essential purchase: Lansdown's high intellectual standard is a gift. For those wanting a salacious taste of his life, again, I recommend: this selection titillates; it thrills. Dip in, with a spit-moistened finger, and find a life lived poetically, a poem lived out in flesh. While Byron's bones lie under the cold stone of Hucknall's St Mary Magdalene Church, his spirit is more vital than ever.

Matt Turpin

CATHERINE MARSHALL
VIOLET TILLARD
JOAN BEAUCHAMP
LYDIA SMITH

Anti-war activists, editors and publishers of the No-Conscription Fellowship 1915-1920

Cranks and Kites

Emily Johns and Gabriel Carlyle, *The World is My Country: A Celebration of the People and Movements that Opposed the First World War in 10 posters and stories*, Peace News Press, 2015, 98 pages, ISBN 9781904527183, £6
Oliver Haslam and PPU Publications Group, *Refusing to Kill: Conscientious Objection and Human Rights in the First World War*, Peace Pledge Union Publications, 2014, 74 pages, ISBN 9780902680524, £10

Two peace-oriented publishers; two different approaches to presenting the lives of conscientious objectors and opponents of the First World War. *The World is My Country* calls itself a 'celebration', whereas *Refusing to Kill* is a more sombre appraisal, and pulls no punches. Read together, they prove there is room to remember both the anguish and the triumphs of this extremely diverse group.

Refusing to Kill is primarily intended for use by teachers and students, as the layout and language indicate. It outlines the various forms of conscientious objection, such as non-combatant COs, who would drill and train but not serve; those who submitted to alternative labour; and absolutists, who opposed the entire system of compulsory service and did not recognise the government's authority to command them to undertake it. The author takes care to unpack the historical and social context around particular conflicts, for example the limited appreciation for what we would now consider 'human rights' as the First World War was brewing. This creates a more rounded impression of what conscientious objectors really opposed, and their unique position. Readers well-versed on the topic might find it repetitive, but I dare say there are useful sections for even the expert.

A particularly valuable passage about the present day suggests that some recruits who go absent without leave from the UK armed forces are unaware that, should they develop moral concerns, they do have the right to stop serving. The words of a deserting paramedic, consumed with doubt after being recalled in 2003 for the Iraq War, confirm the fact:

> 'I never heard the words [conscientious objection]. People think I should have known about it, but there are officers who have been in the RAF twenty years who don't know about it.'

How could such a fundamental right go unheard? In some other countries there is still no provision for conscientious objection – oughtn't we

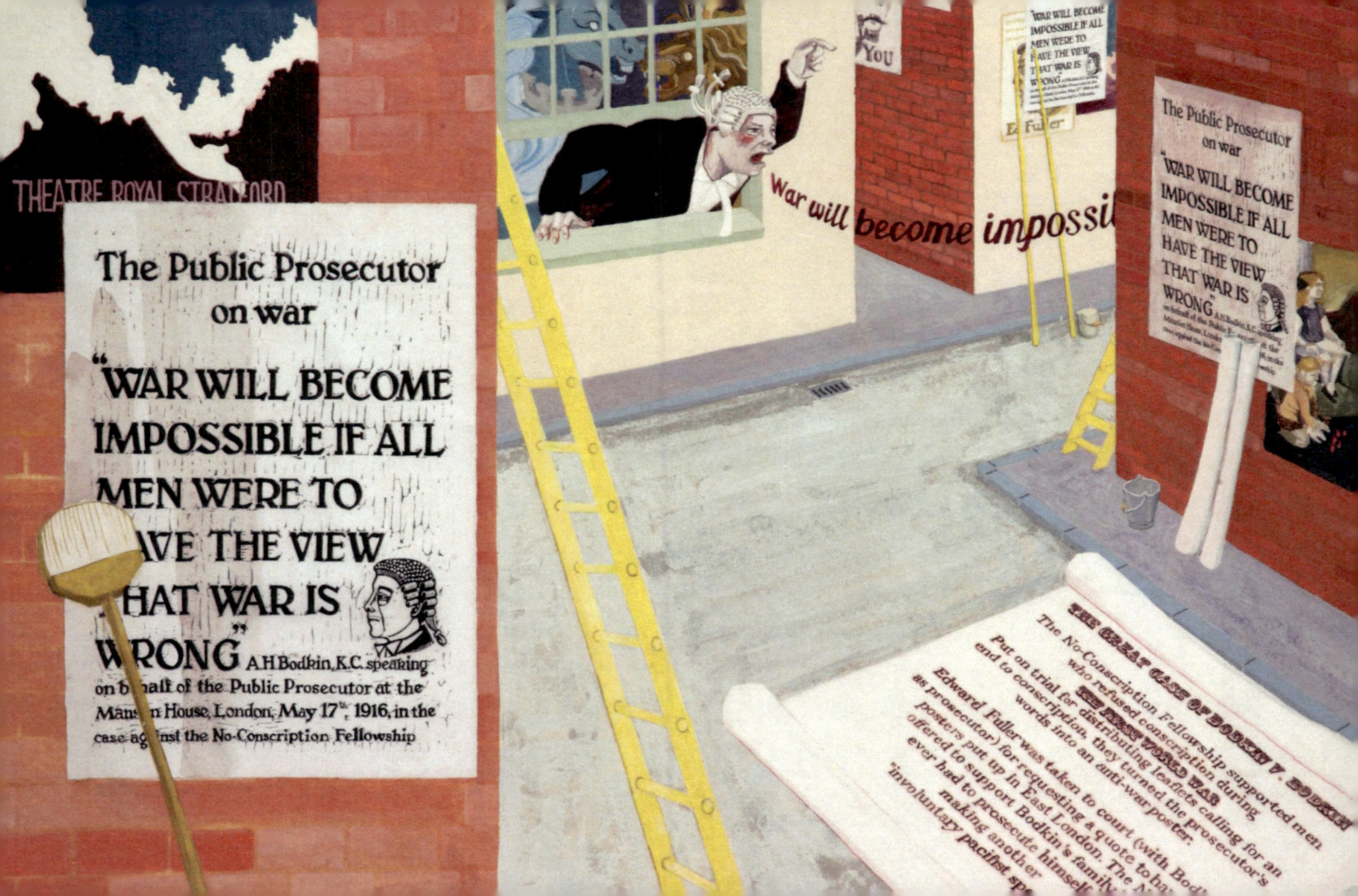

THEATRE ROYAL STRATFORD
The Public Prosecutor
on war
"WAR WILL BECOME
IMPOSSIBLE IF ALL
MEN WERE TO
AVE THE VIEW
HAT WAR IS
WRONG" A.H.Bodkin, K.C. speaking
half of the Public Prosecutor at the
House, London, May 17th, 1916, in the
case against the No-Conscription Fellowship
War will become impossi
YOU
WAR WILL BECOME
IMPOSSIBLE IF ALL
MEN WERE TO
HAVE THE VIEW
THAT WAR IS
WRONG
Fuller
The Public Prosecutor
on war
"WAR WILL BECOME
IMPOSSIBLE IF ALL
MEN WERE TO
HAVE THE VIEW
THAT WAR IS
WRONG"
THE GREAT CASE OF BODKIN V. BODKIN
The No-Conscription Fellowship supported men
who refused conscription during
THE FIRST WORLD WAR
Put on trial for distributing leaflets calling for an
end to conscription, they turned the prosecutor's
words into an anti-war poster.
Edward Fuller was taken to court (with
as prosecutor) for requesting a quote to
posters put up in East London. The
offered to support Bodkin's family
ever had to prosecute himself
making another
"involuntary pacifist

champion the fact that we are permitted this freedom? There can be no conceivable benefit to the government in wasting time and resources sentencing AWOL service members if simple changes to briefing procedures can be made.

Other troubling case studies include the trial of an objector to the Iraq War, who was court-martialled following the decision that his objection was 'political' and therefore invalid. This was despite the fact that 'selective objection' has been recognised in Britain since 1940, and that the individual was willing to serve as an unarmed paramedic. Depressingly, it would seem that even now it is hard to secure a mutually agreed period of conscientious exemption – the fickle spirit of the old tribunals lives on.

To switch tack, and book, *The World is My Country* covers the historical and geopolitical context of the First World War as well, but its vignettes about pacifist personalities are its treasures. We are gently reminded that peace activists – and indeed, those they oppose – are also allowed to engage each other with a sense of humour. A prime example, 'The great case of Bodkin v. Bodkin', concerns a government lawyer's offhand remark that, unbeknownst to him, had made its way onto a No-Conscription Fellowship poster, and been exhibited around the streets of London in late 1916. The genesis of this unusual scenario was the trial of eight members of the NCF earlier the same year, for printing an anti-conscription leaflet. At this trial the prosecutor, Crown Advocate Archibald Bodkin, issued the soon-to-be fateful words 'War will become impossible if all men were to have the view that war is wrong'. The story continues:

> 'Believing that Bodkin had 'kindly provided us with such a terse and explicit phrase, expressing our view regarding war', the NCF mischievously turned Bodkin's unwitting 'pacifist speech' into a poster, and had copies printed by the National Labour Press.'

One Edward Fuller came a cropper of the law when the War Office learned he was seeking a quote for the poster. Bodkin served as prosecutor at the ensuing trial, during which a War Office senior official had to admit the quote was 'perfectly true'; 'a platitude'. Fuller was convicted and fined, but on a positive note the poster's text received a great deal of public exposure.

To further rub Bodkin's nose in it, the NCF's newspaper, the *Tribunal,* pledged that if he 'decide[d] in his devotion to duty to prosecute himself' that they would offer their assistance to his dependents 'should they be threatened with financial or other difficulty as a result of his persecution at the hands of the State or himself'.

We also discover people like Frances Sheehy-Skeffington, who steered himself by the causes of feminism, pacifism, socialism and Irish nationalism. His section contains one of those comebacks you only wish you'd be quick enough to fire off yourself: some considered him a crank, and he was not displeased at this, for 'a crank is a small instrument that makes revolutions'.

It seems Sheehy-Skeffington was a lone voice railing against war amid the mass enlistment of his countrymen. The 1916 Easter Rising saw him apprehended by the British military, against the likes of whom he did not seem to bear a grudge, for we are told

> 'he had braved a hail of bullets to try to rescue a wounded British soldier, explaining: "I could not let anyone bleed to death while I could still help".'

Two days after this selfless act, he was executed.

As one might expect, the authors also cherry-pick some of Bertrand Russell's many exploits. It is Russell's ill-timed banning order that comes up, and how some lectures he had planned to give found an audience even despite him being banned from effectively a third of the country. Found guilty of 'making statements likely to prejudice recruiting', he was prohibited to 'reside in or enter' particular areas as defined under the Aliens Restrictions Act 1914. In body, he apparently obeyed – yet in voice he travelled widely indeed. A few months later Robert Smillie, President of the Miners' Federation of Great Britain, began to deliver one of Russell's lectures to an immense crowd at a Glasgow protest meeting. Unaware at first, those gathered were delighted when he revealed the ruse.

Russell also appears in *Refusing to Kill*, but Catherine Marshall, his comrade in the No-Conscription Fellowship, is given a touch more limelight, in a chapter dedicated to the women's peace movement. There is a particularly nice account of her sending imprisoned COs secret messages, by arranging for children to get white kites 'caught' in a certain tree outside the jail. This was to signal to them that the No-Conscription Fellowship – from whom the prisoners had sought advice – wished for them not to revolt against the prison rules. A signal in red rather than white would have signalled that they *should*.

This pair of texts makes a fine and comprehensive overview of the subject. Comparisons in *Refusing to Kill* between the public view of conscientious objection in the First World War and in modern conflicts show how far we have come, and how much there is yet to achieve. For instance, we could scarcely conceive of conscientious objectors today being disenfranchised, but those of the First World War were – some up until August 1926. This was possibly the least of the indignities COs endured. Many of the punishments listed in the book amount to torture – not only physically brutalised in prison, but starved of human connection in many cases. All this, not for killing, but refusing to kill.

A stand-out sentence in *Refusing to Kill*'s ultimate analysis is that 'Britain did not deal with its own militarism', and so much of the heroics of WWI were in fact futile gestures – more conflict was born out of the loose ends. If only we could say what a difference 100 years makes.

Nicole Morris

Something better

Andrew Bibby, *All Our Own Work: The co-operative pioneers of Hebden Bridge and their mill*, Merlin Press, 2015, 238 pages, paperback ISBN 9780850367102, £15.95

The publication of any book on the UK co-operative movement is a rare event and one to be welcomed. A book about a co-operative of workers and their 'productive society' is especially welcome. This is a sector of the movement which has been represented by hundreds of such societies but hitherto has been disregarded by historians, even by those with an interest in co-operatives. Andrew Bibby's book brings to life the day to day problems, failures and successes of the UK's largest ever 'productive society' – or 'worker co-op' as we might call it today – the Hebden Bridge Fustian Manufacturing Society.

The society was formed in 1870, after Joseph Greenwood and fellow delegates from the local store society, the Hebden Bridge Industrial Co-operative Society, attended the Co-operative Congress in Manchester. Within three months their new fustian (coarse cotton) society was up and running, and within a year had 112 members and was employing 17 of them in fustian cutting. The author follows their every move, from cutting to dyeing, making clothes, and, eventually, to controlling the whole process from the water in their own reservoir that powered the machinery at the Nutclough Mill, to the supply of products to co-operative societies and other customers throughout Britain.

This is not just a business history. The Fustian Society was from its beginning committed to promoting education and, in the 1880s, was paying almost all the costs of holding free lectures by academics from Oxford University, which were attended by as many as 700 people. From these beginnings the Fustian Society was instrumental in the development of the University Extension Movement and the Workers' Educational Association (WEA). This developed from a village with a population of just a few thousand.

The co-operators of Hebden Bridge were also in at the beginning of the Women's Co-operative Guild, having the distinction of setting up the Guild's first branch in 1883. The International Co-operative Alliance also owes much to Hebden Bridge co-operators in its early years. It is one of the strengths of *All Our Own Work* that it examines the development of co-operative ideas and philosophies among the society's leading figures and how, from the Fustian Society, emerged co-operators with clear principles and extended visions, several of whom went on to hold influential positions in the Co-operative Wholesale Society (CWS), the Co-operative Union, and the Co-operative Productive Federation.

Andrew Bibby does not present the history as one of interrupted successes in an onward and upward march of progress. He looks critically at decisions the society made in its early years which affected its relationships with workers and with other co-operative societies in particular; with its sometimes difficult relations with trade unions in the period following the 'new unionism' of the 1890s; the lack of women on the society's committees and delegations; the lack of clear evidence that Nutclough workers were materially better off from being co-operative employees than of any other local employer; and the long running debates about the 'bounty to labour' and the rival claims of the 'workerist' and 'consumerist' co-operative advocates.

The voices of the men and women who worked in the mill are few and far between, but that is unfortunately true of most histories of working class life in this period. We do, however, have several accounts of the society's history written by Greenwood himself, and many other sources which Andrew has used extensively. Had the society survived as a productive society for two more years there would doubtless have been a jubilee history, published in 1920 to mark their 50th year, and Joseph Greenwood, then aged 87, might well have been its author. I have no doubt that he would have approved of Andrew Bibby's questioning but affectionate approach.

This is not just a readable and fascinating history, but also a well-timed account of dilemmas that new co-operatives still have to face, especially those in the worker co-op sector and in the various hybrid co-operatives that have emerged in recent years. The failures at the Co-operative Bank and the Co-operative Group have severely dented the confidence of many co-operators, but the growth of the worker co-op sector and new co-ops in sustainable energy are now emerging as a new force in the movement. May there be many more books like this one to show us how co-operators of the past dealt with their dilemmas so that, in Greenwood's words, 'out of their imperfect society something better in the future might evolve'.

Christopher Richardson

A bookseller in Venice

The return of Marxism? I keep reading about it, yet the radical bookshop where I work has a solitary copy of *Capital* volume one which has been snoozing away gently for two years (and nobody has ever ordered the other volumes). The Venice Biennale, which attracts tens of thousands of artie fartie people from all over the world, chose, this year, to be more political and a showpiece was the daily reading from *Capital* in the main performance space. There it was then, the *Capital Oratorio*, where two professionals used up a fair amount of the Biennale ticket price reading aloud ... reading, when I was there, economic equations, to a house that started off small and, within minutes, had shrunk to me and two Chinese students checking their emails. And then only to the two Chinese students.

I found this year's Biennale rather dull. It's a bit of a problem with installation art which is basically trying to be socialist and cutting edge without presenting a succession of images of people being horrible to other people. Or at least it was here, representing the theme of *All the World's Futures*. The previous Biennale managed to summarise such politics really well with the now famous Jeremy Deller picture of William Morris rising up out of the sea and sinking one of the rich people's mega yachts which had been dominating the shoreline.

Naturally, there is the usual wtf artspeak descriptions of things and plenty opportunities to say 'what, really?' such as the pavilion whose art installation is that the ceiling is painted black and is otherwise completely empty. The British pavilion was painted a gorgeous yellow and I'd have been happier if it had remained empty rather than filled with Sarah Lucas's blow up torsos and plaster casts of the lower half of some of her mates, naked and with cigarettes sticking out of their assorted orifices. *All the world's future's?* Maybe.

There were surprises – like the Congolese artists who try to keep alive the ideas of the Situationist International, but the best pavilion was one made of glass whose entire exhibition was of itself being shattered and, inside, nothing but large broken frames of glass. It could be seen in 30 seconds and *Kristalnacht* came to mind at once. To be fair, there were playful aspects on the site – three entire French trees which moved around slowly on unseen platforms and, from Japan, a delightful installation by Chiharu Shiota of a room full of red yarn from which hung keys, drifting down to two rowing boats below. I am sure there was a deeper, solemn meaning, but to me it was just a thing of beauty.

The best saved itself to last, by chance, as it is easy to wander from pavilion to pavilion at the main, Giardini, site, randomly. A Polish opera company was filmed performing *Halka*, the Polish national opera, in the open air to impoverished villagers in Haiti. One girl had brought her goat with her to the performance, occasionally a dog would walk through the set, and once or twice – it was performed at a crossroads – a bemused lad on a motorbike would sail through. Why there? That village is inhabited by the descendants of Polish soldiers who deserted from the French army in the first decade of the nineteenth century to join the Haitian resistance and became stranded. Even now the villagers include people who are nearly white and have sort of Polish names. One of the themes of the Biennale is 'identity'. I have no idea what the Haitians thought of these people coming there to perform, but colonialism is like that – we go there, they come here, and things are never the same.

If the Giardini is not enough, the contrasting Arsenale site comprises a long series of interlinked rooms, once the site of a ship-building factory. In the *London Review of Books* Alice Sprawls referred to the space here as unrelenting at the best of times (though I did not find it so previously) and I walked through the aisles stunned. This was art as a machine, grinding into your brain forever. You had to be there to understand. It was a relief to find one of the last exhibition rooms where Mozambique had forgotten the rules and had a small exhibition of the country's literature, music and folk art, suitable for any classroom trip.

Back in Venice itself, all the world's futures continue to collide with the right-wing mayor banning a gay pride march and continuing to welcome cruise ships the size of a small nation state, whose visits are destroying the canals and local ecology.

Ross Bradshaw
www.fiveleavesbookshop.co.uk